11. AUG 02.

01. DEC 12.

1 0 FEB 2011

03 SEP 2016

OSIDGE LIBRARY
020 8359 3920

Please return/renew this item by the
last date shown to avoid a charge.
Books may also be renewed by phone
and Internet. May not be renewed if
required by another reader.

www.libraries.barnet.gov.uk

D1421273

30131 04449002 2

London Borough of Barnet

Goodbye Dear Friend

Goodbye Dear Friend

Coming to Terms with
The Death of a Pet

Virginia Ironside

BOOKS

For Laelia in memory of Basil

London Borough of Barnet	
Askews	Apr-2009
155.937	£12.99

First published in Great Britain in 2009 by
JR Books, 10 Greenland Street, London NW1 0ND

Copyright © 2009 Virginia Ironside

Virginia Ironside has asserted her moral right to be identified as the Author of this Work in accordance with the Copyright Designs and Patents Act 1988.

All rights reserved. No part of this book may be reproduced or utilised in any form or by any means, electronic or mechanical, including photocopying, recording or by any information storage and retrieval system, without permission in writing from JR Books.

A catalogue record for this book is available from the British Library.

ISBN 978-1-906217-93-8

1 3 5 7 9 10 8 6 4 2

Printed in by MPG Books, Bodmin, Cornwall

Contents

Introduction

When you choose a pet to share your life, you're getting companionship, love, devotion and unswerving loyalty. However, you're also getting something else. You're getting its death. Pets live such short lives compared with us, that pet lovers will probably own at least three or four in their lifetime. And they will probably have to suffer the grief of losing them all.

Unless you're an animal lover, it's difficult to understand how deeply pet death can affect owners. Because, since grief is the price we pay for loving, you have to first understand about loving an animal. And there's a kind of taboo about admitting strong affection for another species. To adore something so fundamentally different is often seen as rather weird.

If I write about child abuse, victims of rape, or battered wives, I'm usually sure to get a small avalanche of letters from people in similar positions. At last, the unspeakable has been brought into the open!

But if I put a letter on the problem page about someone who is unhappy over the death of an animal, that small avalanche turns into a huge one. Hundreds and hundreds and hundreds of people write in, pouring their hearts out. They speak of the dreadful grief that they, too, have felt when a pet has died; but what they really speak of is love – a love they feel they can't share fully with other people, because it is love not for a fellow human, but an animal.

'Sympathy with the lower animals is one of the noblest virtues with which man is endowed,' said Charles Darwin. And yet anyone who loves animals enormously is seen as a little bit cracked. The crazy English ladies who feed the strays cats in Naples; the loopy widow who left all her money to Battersea Dogs & Cats Home; the man who killed himself when his budgie died; the tourist who spends £800 on quarantine fees to bring back a stray dog who'd adopted her in Spain – they're thought all very sad and touching, but completely bonkers!

I wonder why it never occurs to people who don't really love animals that it is *they* who are the crazy ones? At some churches occasional services are held for animal blessings. 'Some say it's very sentimental and some say there's no point in blessing an animal,' says the former Bishop of Salisbury. 'But the beauty of the life and character of an animal is a blessing in itself. We should get blessed by animals rather than the other way round.'

Whenever I've talked about writing this book, people have been fascinated – and fascinated in a way that makes it obvious that the subject taps into something deep within us. The responses have varied from floods of tears from one girl who fled the room at the very mention of the subject of pet bereavement because it reminded her of how strongly she had felt when her cat had died, to, more commonly, the over-hysterical hoots of laughter when I tell of the lady who has a shrine to her guinea pig.

Why should we feel that it's only our own species that deserve our love? What on earth makes us feel that we are so special? Those of us who do love animals usually hide the nature of our love so successfully, even sometimes from ourselves, that it's small wonder we feel, when our pets die, that we have to hide or diminish our grief in front of others. And small wonder that some of us find it difficult to deal with. Small wonder, too, that I had such an amazing response when I asked for contributions to this book.

I hope that by reading of others' experiences – from ordinary people today to Freud and Sir Walter Scott – we can understand that it's those of us who can love animals who are the lucky ones – even if the price is a grief, when they die, that may seem, at times, overwhelming.

Chapter 1

‹〰›

Our Relationship with Pets

'The greatest pleasure of a dog is that you may make a fool
of yourself with him and not only will he not scold you
but he will make a fool of himself, too.'

Samuel Butler

W hat do most of us love about animals? The fact that they
don't speak is certainly part of their appeal. They're
never going to nag us or criticise us. They're also totally
uninhibited. They will leap, growl, drool and roll wherever they are.
And, thirdly, unlike children they never leave home and become
independent.

Jerome K. Jerome, author of *Three Men in a Boat* brilliantly summed
up our feelings for pets in the following:

I like cats and dogs very much indeed. What jolly chaps
they are! They are much superior to human beings as
companions. They do not quarrel or argue with you. They
never talk about themselves but listen to you while you
talk about yourself, and keep up an appearance of being

interested in the conversation. They never say unkind things. They never tell us of our faults 'merely for our own good'. They do not, at inconvenient moments, remind us of our past follies and mistakes. They never inform us that we are not nearly so nice as we used to be. We are always the same to them. They are always glad to see us. They are with us in all our humours. They are merry when we are glad, sober when we feel solemn, sad when we are sorrowful . . .

And when we bury our face in our hands and wish we had never been born, they don't sit up very straight, and observe that we have brought it all upon ourselves. They don't even hope it will be a warning to us.

But they come up softly and shove their heads against us. If it is a dog, he looks up at you with his big, true eyes, and says with them, 'Well, you've always got me, you know. We'll go through the world together, and always stand by each other, won't we?'

He is very imprudent, a dog is. He never makes it his business to inquire whether you are in the right or in the wrong, never bothers as to whether you are going up or down upon life's ladder, never asks whether you are rich or poor, silly or wise, sinner or saint. Come luck or misfortune, good repute or bad, honour or shame, he is going to stick to you, to comfort you, guard you, and give his life for you, if need be . . . You are his pal. That is enough for him.

Okay, you might say. That's basically it. He's said it all. Next chapter, please. But while many people love their pets for the fundamental baseline qualities that Jerome K. Jerome describes, there are also other important aspects to their relationships. I must emphasise that these are not the fundamental reasons for loving them, they are bonuses, in the same way a woman might love her husband as a person, but also loves him because he's rich, strong and good looking. Were he to become poor, ugly and disabled she would still love him, but that doesn't mean she can't enjoy the other things he gives her while he's on the up as well. So, pet owners may relate to their pets as:

Protectors

As well as being pets, dogs are often used to guard their owners and their owners' property as well. They make them feel safe at night.

Signs of sexuality

We've all seen minuscule men walking down the street hanging on to enormous slobbering dogs. You don't have to be Freud to know what the dog signifies. Similarly, the simpering lady who cuddles a much-loved poodle is using her dog rather like lipstick, to show she's feminine.

Status symbols

A very fancy dog or cat can be rather like a Mercedes – a signal that one is well-off or ahead of the times. Because they were fashionable at the time I had him, I was inordinately, snobbishly and pathetically proud of my cat who was half a Maine Coon. I should emphasise here that this pride was quite separate from my love for him as a cat.

Children

Many people, with or without children, use their pets as a surrogate family. This is the artist Tracey Emin, talking about her cat, Docket:

I should be feeling secure and comfortable, but instead I am filled with fear. As I lie out in the sun, tears burn my eyes as I recount in my mind the last eight years of my life. Today I was given the news that Docket, my cat, has contracted feline Aids (otherwise known as FIV). Docket is not just a pet to me. Without sounding too corny, he is really like my baby. I constantly say this. I love him more than anything else in the world. I love his yellow eyes, his big ears, his white paws with puffy pink pads, his fluffy white tummy and soft grey fur. But most of all, I love his warmth, and I love his smell. When I cuddle him I rest my face on top of his head and remind myself of how much I love him.

The reason why I love him so much is because of all the love I have invested into him. To some people a cat is just a cat. It miaows, it has to be fed, and it has a tail. But for me, cats are small animals which occupy a massive amount of my mind – especially Docket, who I live with. If I'm honest, I realise that I plan a lot of my life around my cat. And by this, I don't mean small things, I mean where I live, who I live with and my future plans. Should I move to the country? Should I live by the sea? Every large-scale decision that I make involves Docket.

Excuses for letting go

The hung-up father who can barely hug his children, let alone kiss his wife in public, often loses all inhibitions with his dog and can drool over it, kiss it and playfully roll around on the floor with it, with no embarrassment at all. Chaps are allowed to behave in completely daft ways with dogs without losing face.

Reminders of a lost relative

Many is the widow or widower who hangs on to the memory of her or his partner through the pet they left behind. It's when that pet dies that the grief is finally vented.

Links with childhood and nature

The marvellous spontaneity of a dog or cat, the charming way they race through the woods, leap up at you with their tongues hanging out, or quite unshyly groom themselves in front of you, is tremendously appealing. Konrad Lorenz, the great ethologist, wrote in 1952: 'The pleasure I derive from my dog is closely akin to the joy accorded to me by the raven, greylag goose or other wild animals that enliven my walks through the countryside; it seems like a re-establishment of the immediate bond with that unconscious omniscience that we call nature.'

Reasons for existence

Many lonely people use their pets as a reason for getting up, getting dressed, going for walks, eating and so on. Without the pet there'd be nothing to live for.

A way to play God

Many breeders who arrange mating, and care for the offspring, feel more than fatherly feelings for their broods. Their pets make them feel almost omnipotent.

Ways of making friends

Dog owners particularly use their pets as 'social facilitators', as they are known. When I dog-sat a friend's dog I was amazed (and rather unnerved) at the number of complete strangers who came up to me and started conversations in the park. Indeed, many is the romance that has been started over a chance meeting in the park accompanied by a couple of dogs.

Only friends

If you are a mad, old alcoholic who lives in a cardboard box, a dog or cat may be the only friend you have. Of course it is just as true that if you are a brilliant, beautiful woman a dog still might be the only friend you have.

Huggables

Cuddling and kissing fur and flesh in a way that's entirely sensual and totally non-sexual is very therapeutic.

The only ones who care

A dog or cat will never pass judgement on you. Children may find pets particularly comforting friends. Even if they have cheated at maths or forgotten to tidy their room, the pet cares not a fig. It just loves.

Objects of spoiling

Some dogs are completely pampered. One who appeared on television wore Chanel No 5, had a four-poster bed, a simulated fur coat and jeans. Another woman gave her two Yorkies their own bedroom. At Christmas they got crackers with squeaky toys in them, doggy chocs, pet horoscopes, Christmas cake with paw-marks on top, doggy shampoo — and one lady had even dyed her dogs different colours.

Family unity

This is what Dr John Brown (1810–1882) said about dogs: 'I think every family should have a dog; it's like having a perpetual baby. It's the plaything and crony of the whole house.'

One of the big drawbacks about pets is their short lifespans. From the beginning we know that unless we are suffering a terminal illness, or are pretty ancient, they're almost certainly going to die before us. Pets, after all, live on average only a fifth of our own lives. As a vet wrote in an article on 'Understanding Animal Death': 'At each first visit I talk about the average life expectancy of the pet. I want them to know at the start. If they walk in with a mouse that's three weeks old, I want them to know that in eighteen months they will have a very old mouse.'

'The misery of keeping a dog is his dying so soon,' wrote Sir Walter Scott. 'But, to be sure, if he lived for fifty years and then died, what would become of me?'

So, from the moment we acquire a pet we are hostages to grief. Is it really worth the agony of suffering the sadness of loss again and again and again?

It seems it is. The love for a pet is crucial for many of us. Surveys show that half of pet owners in the US and Britain keep pictures of their pets either in their wallets (or on mobile phones) or on their walls, half allow them to sleep with them or a member of the family and nearly 80 per cent of respondents in a survey carried out by *Psychology Today* said that at some time their pet had been their closest companion.

> The lady that bought him (a dog) for me died and some nights I would go to bed and lay there thinking of her and would cry – I had to give vent to my emotions. And Rusty would sense this because when I sniffed he would jump up on my bed, offer me his paw and then start to whine. I said: 'Don't worry, Rusty,' and he would then settle down, ears pricked. I am a bachelor but have many brothers and sisters, mates and friends but I get enough companionship from Rusty and my other dog, Mickey.
>
> David

And this account came from a woman who had temporarily split up with her husband:

> Our dog was even closer to me than before. He knew there was something wrong. He used to sit and listen when I was upset. Then the big cold nose would sniff my cheek as if to say: 'I'm here, you'll be all right.'

This sad letter was written by a soldier in the First World War:

> I found him in a dug-out on the old Somme battlefield, half-starved, and since then he has shared my meals and also my blankets at night. He is such a faithful companion and guard I cannot think of leaving him behind when I return to Blighty. He has been a faithful animal to me both in holding and attacking. I have had him about twelve months and he was with me all through the retirement of 1918, and with me through the late attacks since August 1918. He has been slightly wounded twice in going over the top with me, but he has been inoculated by a friend on the RAMC each time. Kindly do your best for me, as I think he deserves to come with me, as he stuck to me through thick and thin, and when I was wounded and could not walk he stayed with me all through the attack under a heavy barrage for nearly three hours, so you can imagine how attached I am to him . . .

But perhaps what people like most about pets is the unconditional love that they give them. Says Suzanne Thomas, a pet bereavement counsellor: 'Pet-owners often experience the kind of love from a pet which they've never experienced from anyone else. For those people it's the most loving relationship they've had. The relationship can go very, very deep with a pet because there are no words – and it's particularly important for those people who are rather inarticulate generally, or withdrawn. But the relationship with a pet can be a prime relationship, even for people who have healthy family relationships, because it can touch something that perhaps nothing else touches. People can be close to an animal in a way that they can't be close to a human being. And pets give us a sense of value. They can give sense and structure to our lives – particularly when we have to rush home to feed them and so on.'

'A dog will never criticise,' says Katie Boyle, who owns four rescued dogs and is involved in many animal charities. 'You can rely on its sympathy. A dog knows when you're sad and will never leave you alone.

'When I was very ill, all that time when I had no energy and was in bed, I had four dogs on the bed. They never left. When they had to go out and were taken for walks, they rushed back. They just said: "We're here, don't worry." Some men feel: "Oh God, what a bore, she's ill"; some friends don't want to hear again what pain you're in and you don't want to bore them. But with a dog you can say to it: "God I feel terrible, thanks for loving me and I do love you."'

To many, their pets mean more to them than their own, close family:

> Why did I break down and suffer more when my beloved Lucy had to be put down than when my parents died? I have thought about this long and hard and all I can come up with is our communication, or lack of it. With humans we can express our thoughts, deeds and feelings because it's easy to communicate. With animals it is very hard. We could never tell Lucy that by cutting down her food and administering pills we were trying to help her. Did she

think we were trying to starve her? Did she understand?
That is what makes her death so painful to me.

Diane

But many appreciate this bond of silence:

There are those among us who will always relate to
animals more than people. I have found that people often
let you down and can cause such misery in one's life. My
animals never do. I am totally at peace when walking
through woods or parks with them. They like me for what
I am and their moods never change.

Tom

Sir Walter Scott didn't let communication bother him. He talked
to his dogs, despite the fact they couldn't reply. He was described,
by one of his friends, like this: 'In our walks he would frequently
pause in conversation to notice his dogs and speak to them as if
rational companions; and indeed there appears to be a vast deal of
rationality in these faithful attendants on man, derived from their
close intimacy with him . . . His domestic animals were his friends.'

Dr Colin Murray-Parkes, a psychiatrist who specialises in
bereavement, says that the object of an attachment to an animal,
apart from as beasts of burden, is a love relationship. 'It may fulfill
your need to have a baby after you've stopped being able to
conceive, or it may give love to those people who can't cope with
the responsibility of making attachments to other human beings.
People who over-invest in pets are people who have for one reason
or another blocked off from other human beings – they've been
betrayed or had poor experiences of parenting themselves. Animals
are less complicated, are easier to comprehend and easier to trust.'

But not all people who love and then grieve bitterly over the loss of an animal are damaged. Many simply find that animals give them more than their fellow men.

In a letter describing his dog, the poet Alexander Pope wrote: 'If it be the chief point of friendship to comply with a friend's notions and inclinations, he possesses this in an eminent degree; he lies down when I sit, and walks when I walk, which is more than many good friends can pretend to.'

And Konrad Lorenz: 'We judge the moral worth of two human friends according to which of them is ready to make the greater sacrifice without thought of recompense. The plain fact that my dog loves me more than I love him is undeniable and always fills me with a certain feeling of shame. The dog is ever ready to lay down his life for me.'

There is, too, a purity about the relationship between owner and pet. Pets can never be sarcastic or ironic. They can never gossip behind your back. They can never pinch your girlfriend. They never have a bigger car than you; they never want to borrow a tenner; they never get pissed and embarrass you; and they never ring you up moaning about their boyfriends. They never ask you if their bums look big in this. They are entirely trustworthy. When most humans die we usually experience ambivalent feelings about them. We may miss their sense of humour but perhaps we're glad to be rid of their back-biting, for example. When an animal dies there's nothing unpleasant to look back on. They have never betrayed us. They can't.

> I never trust anyone who doesn't like dogs and I have
> never met a dog I didn't like. The only thing I ever liked
> about Hitler was his love for Blondi.
>
> Peter

Even Freud spotted in himself a weakness for dogs – and noticed why. 'It really explains why one can love an animal like Topsy (or

Jo-fi) with such an extraordinary intensity; affection without ambivalence, the simplicity of life free from the almost unbearable conflicts of civilisation, the beauty of an existence complete in itself. And yet, despite all divergence in the organic development, the feeling of an intimate affinity, of an undisputed solidarity. Often when stroking Jo-fi I have caught myself humming a melody which, unmusical as I am, I can't help recognising as the aria from *Don Giovanni*: "A bond of friendship Unites us both . . ."'

While some use their pets as their friends, others see them as their children. In one survey, nine out of ten people considered the pet a member of their family, and the majority of people answered 'child' when asked: 'Which kind of family member does your pet resemble?'

According to the vet, Dr Bruce Fogle, we humanise pets more than we used to. Dogs used to be called Rover, Spot, Shep, Bone – doggy names. Today males are most likely to be called Max and females, Molly.

But this description shows clearly how a couple relate to their dog as a human being:

> As our Yorkshire terrier settled in, his character started to show. He was so stubborn! He would dig his little heels in and would not do something if he didn't want to.
>
> When he did do as he was told, his little tail would go and his ears cock up. 'Aren't I a good boy?' was what he was saying, 'Aren't I clever?' I forgot he was a naughty boy and would make such a fuss of him, you would have thought he had done something magnificent, he'd only obeyed me! When I was busy, usually in the morning doing housework or at the kitchen sink, he would tip up his toy-box, get out his tinkly rubber bone or his squeaky carrot, his favourite toys, and throw them at my feet. 'Come on, mum, leave that,

play with me,' he seemed to say, his little tail going nineteen to the dozen, his ears stuck up, his head cocked to one side, I couldn't resist him! 'Walkies' was his favourite word. He would bark and race round, unless of course it was raining or very windy, then his tail and head would go down, he would stand still and ignore calls to 'come on'. 'Bed' was another favourite word, he would run up the stairs, stand by our bed and wait to be picked up and for us to move the top pillow away from the headboard, so he could sleep on the bottom pillow. He would wait for his dad to come up and bring his cup of tea.

When we had the shop he soon got to know the voices of the people who would make a fuss of him. He would come out of the back room and sit by the door (he knew he was not allowed in the shop) his little tail going, his ears cocked up, and the person was always enchanted with him. Sometimes he would cautiously come and whine because he knew we sold doggie chews in the shop. 'What's mummy got?' I would say as I gave him one. 'Little Bouncelot' is what his dad called him. When his dad got back from work he would always be waiting, dancing up and down until his dad bounced him.

This comes from a librarian who went a stage further.

My cocker spaniel was such a good friend, listening to my troubles, never passing judgement, always there with a comforting lick. When she was younger she bit one of my children who was teasing her and the doctor suggested having her put down. But I said I'd rather see my child put down.

Clive Jackman, who started the Cambridge Pet Crematorium, pointed out that while children leave you, pets stay for ever. 'Look, you might have a son. He might emigrate to Australia in ten years' time, marry a lovely little lady and have children. And it might be that you find yourself, here in this country, as happens to thousands of people, alone with your dog. But your dog never goes away. Your cat never goes away. Your pet is with you from the moment you get it to the moment it dies. It might mean more at that moment to the owner than the actual son or daughter. I worry about all my children, even mine in Australia. But anything could be happening to them now — I just don't know about it. But my dog — he's down the corridor. This is what people don't understand.'

Pets are also good for us, apparently — another reason we might mourn them if they go, even if we're only subconsciously aware of the role they play in keeping us healthy. Dr James Serpell of the Companion Animal Research Group at Cambridge University was quoted as saying: 'There is evidence that people are more relaxed in the company of animals than they are with other humans, but nobody really understands why yet. It's not as simple as people being calmed down by stroking animals because they seem to have the same effect if they are just in the room.'

Research has shown in a ten-month health study that within weeks of their dog's or cat's arrival, 50 per cent of owners were reporting fewer minor health problems such as headaches, coughs, colds, tiredness, indigestion or nerves.

Further evidence of the benefits on health of owning a pet appears in the *Medical Journal of Australia*. In screening tests on 5,741 people of all ages attending a health clinic it was found that those who owned pets had lower blood pressures. Pet owners also took more exercise.

I always think that there is very little difference in the
feelings of loss of a human or a pet — and the answer is
always to get a replacement — of either! The therapeutic
value of stroking a pet is wonderful for the owner and the
pet (come to that, my husband, who is a very hairy man,
loves being stroked and having his tummy tickled!).

Dolores

What about small animals? While most people, even those who
don't own pets, can identify up to a point with the kinds of feelings
people have for cats and dogs, it stretches many people's
imaginations to realise that such feelings may extend to rats,
hamsters or guinea pigs. But one middle-aged guinea-pig owner was
bereft when her pet died of an injection of anaesthetic at the vet
when he was in for a minor dental procedure:

Frankly I was devastated. I loved him and that's that. If it's
got fur and four legs I'm a sucker. If you have a pet it's
part of the family. Guinea pigs are regarded as child's toys
— the vet said you wouldn't have a guinea pig unless you
were ten — but any animal is a little thing in its own right.
Perhaps it's because I live alone, or because I'm childless,
but I was beside myself. I missed him and saw him in every
corner. Some friends bought me another guinea pig — but
there's no replacing him really. He died six months ago. I
feel so guilty, I had only taken him for his front teeth to
be clipped — then the vet said the back ones had to be
done. He rang me and said my guinea pig was fine,
recovering nicely — and then he died. I'm still finding out
about the stuff he was given to see if he should have had
this particular injection.

I've had three guinea pigs in all. The first one died naturally. I was upset but not as upset as this one. The next one was Tiggy, he lived six years. I cared for him, I had hoped he'd live longer than the average.

This last knew me very well. He could distinguish me from other people and I appreciated it. I felt flattered. I chatted silly talk to him, he snuggled down and listened and seemed to know me. That guinea pig trusted me. They have more upstairs than ever we dream of, more upstairs than us, certainly.

What about rats? 'I have come across some people who really don't have any other pets or anything like that and their rat or rats are the main abiding thing in their lives,' says Nick Mays, past president of the National Fancy Rat Society. 'I have seen people very depressed when they've lost an animal. Sometimes it's very difficult for other people to understand. I don't mock people who get upset when a pet dies. Rats are very intelligent and certainly capable of feeling affection and giving affection to their human owners.

'When I was ten I kept tadpoles; one became a froglet and died. I got hysterical about it, partly because he was dead and partly because it was my fault because I hadn't built him a platform. They say a frog is just a bag of nervous responses but I don't really believe that.'

Dr Mary Stewart, who used to work at the Veterinary School of the University of Glasgow, recalled an animal nurse who grieved for a small animal: 'When her hamster died she came in in tears. He used to follow her around in his exercise ball.

'When vets are concerned and go to a lot of trouble over something small and apparently worthless, people are overly grateful.'

As us agony aunts are used to saying, size really doesn't matter. Many of us adore our animals, be they ugly and smelly or fluffy and pretty, tiny or huge. We often love them more than human beings. And, as we will see from the next chapter, we are devastated when they die.

Elegy on the Death of Bingo Our Trench Dog

Weep, weep, ye dwellers in the delved earth,
Ah, weep, ye watchers by the dismal shore
Of No Man's Land, for Bingo is no more;
He is no more, and well we knew his worth,
For whom on bully beefless days were kept
Rare bones by each according to his means,
And while the Quartermaster-Sergeant slept,
The elusive pork was rescued from the beans.
He is no more and, imprudently brave
The loathly rats sit grinning on his grave.

Him mourn the grimy cocks and bombers ten,
The sentinels in lonely posts forlorn,
The fierce patrols with hands and tunics torn,
The furtive band of sanitary men
The murmuring sound of grief along the length
Of traversed trench the startled Hun could hear;
The Captain, as he struck him off the strength,
Let fall a sad and solitary tear;
'Tis even said a batman passing by
Had seen the Sergeant-Major wipe his eye.

The fearful fervour of the feline chase
He never knew, poor dog, he never knew;
Content with optimistic zeal to woo
Reluctant rodents in this murky place,
He never played with children on clean grass
Nor dozed at ease beside the flowing embers,
Nor watched with hopeful eye the tea-cakes pass,
Nor smelt the heather-smell of Scotch Septembers,

For he was born amid a world at war
Although unrecking what we struggled for.

Yet who shall say that Bingo was unblest
Though all his Spratless life was passed beneath
The roar of mortars and the whistling breath
Of grim nocturnal heavies going West?
Unmoved he heard the evening hymn of hate,
Unmoved would gaze into his master's eyes,
For all the sorrows men for men create
In search of happiness, wise dogs despise.
Finding ecstatic joy in every rag
And every smile of friendship worth a wag.

Major E. De Stein

My Cat and Dog

Why come they not? They do not come
My breaking heart to meet;
A heavier darkness on me falls
I cannot lift my feet.

Oh, yes, they come — they never fail
To listen for my sighs;
My poor heart brightens when it meets
The sunshine of their eyes.

Again they come to meet me — God!
Wilt thou the thought forgive?
If 'twere not for my cat and dog
I think I could not live . . .

Ebenezer Elliott, (19th Century)

The Power of the Dog

There is sorrow enough in the natural way
From men and women to fill our day;
And when we are certain of sorrow in store
Why do we always arrange for more?
Brothers and Sisters, I bid you beware
Of giving your heart to a dog to tear.

Buy a pup and your money will buy
Love unflinching that cannot lie —
Perfect passion and worship fed
By a kick in the ribs or a pat on the head.
Nevertheless it is hardly fair
To risk your heart for a dog to tear.

When the fourteen years which Nature permits
Are closing in asthma, or tumour, or fits,
And the vet's unspoken prescription runs
To lethal chambers or loaded guns,
There you will find — it's your own affair —
But . . . you've given your heart to a dog to tear.

When the body that lived at your single will,
With its whimper of welcome is stilled (how still)
When the spirit that answered your every mood
Is gone — wherever it goes — for good,
You will discover how much you care
And will give your heart to a dog to tear.

We've sorrow enough in the natural way,
When it comes to burying Christian clay

Our loves are not given, but only lent,
At compound interest of cent per cent.
Though it is not always the case, I believe,
That the longer we've kept 'em, the more do we grieve;
For, when debts are payable, right or wrong,
A short-time loan is as bad as a long —
So why in Heaven (before we are there)
Should we give our hearts to a dog to tear?

                                    Rudyard Kipling

Chapter 2

⬖

Grieving

'I marched round the house and garden, crying out and
cursing God. It was a terribly sunny day . . . Then I threw
away his big sack of special avocado-based dry food and
all his rubber balls except the red one with the bell inside. I
also kept a lead. When I called Regina and said his name I
broke down and cried. For the first time in ages. I dreamt
that Beefy's double was romping up and down the many
floors of my house, chasing the red ball.'

Ian Whitcomb, *Resident Alien*

In our society we are very hard on those who grieve over losses.
If we feel depressed for longer than a month about the death of
a close relative we're thought a bit odd; if we feel low over the
loss of a necklace or a treasured possession we are thought to be
unpleasantly materialistic; grieving over a pet is, usually, thought to
be so bizarre as to be funny.

As we saw in the last chapter, losing a pet can mean the loss of
many other things. But then losing a husband can also mean losing
other things as well – money, status, sex and so on. So the fact that

we loved a pet partly because of the protection he offered us, or the sensual feelings he gave us, in no way invalidates any of our pain.

Where grief over a pet differs over grief over the death of a human being is that, like the love we had for it, the grief is pure. It's unlikely we will have had a row with our pet just before it died. Unlikely, too, that there are aspects of its character that we found treacherous or unacceptable and which makes us, in one sense, relieved that it has gone. And from the people I've talked to and the letters I've received, I've been astonished at how deep people's feelings are following the death of a pet.

Many doctors and psychiatrists, and even bereavement counsellors, seem unaware of the grief that some people suffer when much-loved animals pass away.

'It's not very often that clients of mine end up in psychiatric hospitals but I think it happens more when the presenting case is animal bereavement than anything else,' says Suzanne Thomas. 'The hidden grief has been so enormous. Life has become so distorted and everywhere they've taken it, it's been dismissed with an "Oh, yes, isn't it sad, oh yes, poor old thing he died, get another one."

'I remember one man whose life completely disintegrated when his dog was run over. He abandoned his business. His wife left him. And every day he would just go and sit by the road where the accident happened and go over and over and over it. Had somebody been around for him at the time it would have been a very tragic and very sad but very straightforward bereavement. But there was nobody. He was referred to me six months after the dog died. But in the end I had to recommend that he went into hospital.

'It is not just other people's fault. The bereaved themselves often feel guilty about grieving for they, too, feel it is "only a pet" and they question whether it is right to have such depth of feelings over an animal.'

I had a beautiful black cat called Smokey. He had a mane
like a lion and a big bushy tail like a fox. He went missing
and I found him dead in a churchyard near my home. I
went through all the stages of grief you feel for a human –
sorrow, anger, regret, guilt. Could I have looked after him
better? Could I have done more to ensure his safety? Had
he been happy? I persecuted myself as to how it had
happened and said a thousand and one times – 'If only . . .'
I still look out of the window for him and when I come
back from shopping I feel so sad as he knew the car and
was always there to greet me. Things have got so bad I am
being treated by the doctor. I have got to the point where I
feel there is no purpose to my life even though I am a
mature student at university.

Emily

Professor Brice Pitt, of the Royal College of Psychiatrists, says:
'I have had experience of people precipitated into depression as a
result of the loss of a pet. In particular with old people, the loss of
a pet seemed to mean a lot more to them when they had already
lost a spouse. Loss of a pet can be a critical factor in serious
depression and the presence of a pet can be a big factor in
preventing the recurrence of depression.'

Clive Jackman, of the Cambridge Pet Crematorium, told this sad
story: 'One fellow contacted me. His parents had both died in the
space of four months, his wife had died a couple of months before,
he had a couple of dogs and one had had to be put down because
it was ill. His whole world had turned upside down after four
months. On top of this he'd been told he had MS and now he
found that his surviving dog would have to be put down because it
had a terrible disease. He asked me to collect it from the vet and he
was there when I arrived. He asked if I would look after the body

as if it were my own dog and I said that of course I would. He then
gave me an envelope and walked away. I said to the vet: "Somebody
ought to watch that fellow." I had this premonition. The letter told
me all stuff about his solicitor and his will and what he wanted
done with the ashes and so on. It was terribly sad. A fortnight later
he committed suicide.'

These two case histories illustrate how upset people can become
when their pet dies:

> I was devastated. It made me really ill as she (her cat,
> Holly) was a child substitute. The suddenness of her death
> had such a profound effect on me I was unable to go to
> work ever again after having an excellent sick record for
> over thirty years. I ended up going to see a psychiatrist and
> even now over a year later I am still attending the hospital
> and still taking anti-depressants.
>
> Brenda

> I didn't think I could ever cry so much (after the death of
> three dogs in quick succession), and the pain in my chest
> made me think I was dying of a heart attack. I couldn't eat
> for the lump in my throat and I couldn't sleep and when I
> did I would imagine that I could feel the dogs getting on
> and off the bed and would move my legs to make room
> for them. I would be standing at the sink and be certain I
> could feel one of them leaning against my leg. I would lock
> myself in the bathroom and break down with such a
> feeling of loss and hurt and even now as I write to you
> almost a year later I am experiencing the same pain. The
> loyalty, love and pleasure those animals gave to us goes
> way beyond words and for all the pain I feel I wouldn't
> have missed one single day with any of them — nor would I

have wished to prolong their time with me when they were in pain and obviously suffering. I wish I could be like those people who accept that a 'dog is a dog and life goes on' but I refuse to apologise to anyone for having the feelings I do. I have just been able to make up a photo collection of the three and I've hung it on the wall for all to see and enjoy. I often talk to them, telling them what's been happening (will they take me away soon to the nut-house?!).

Nancy

Professor Elaine Murphy, a psychiatrist at Guy's Hospital, was quoted as saying: 'From time to time one certainly does come across people who have developed quite a severe depressive illness as a result of losing a pet. It seems to me that it is due to the affection one invests in an animal rather than the affection one gets back.'

From time to time? The more I researched the subject of grief, the more I discovered what an enormous number of people there are whose domestic and working lives have been completely disrupted by depression sparked off by the death of an animal. But often they never even get to the doctor. They are too ashamed.

One study carried out by an American grief counsellor in which pet owners were asked whether the loss of their pet had affected their health showed that 50 per cent of women said yes – while only 15 per cent of men said the same.

One lady, who had looked after her grandmother's dog periodically and thought she had got over its death quite easily, suddenly became 'listless, lethargic, didn't want to eat, lost weight dramatically and became so ill that I had to go to the local hospital for tests. They explored all possible causes and drew a blank. Eventually, after about six months, a doctor suggested I might be grieving over a family loss or that of a loved pet. He had, of course, hit the nail on the head. It had never occurred to me that Gin's death had affected me so much and once I had accepted this I slowly recovered.'

Grief seems to hit owners with even more severity if they have 'rescued' an animal. In a study of 52 adults quoted by Dr Mary Stewart she says that the conclusions showed that 'being responsible for the animal during its life seemed to make the owner feel responsible for its death as well'.

'A friend of mine rescued a fox cub once,' says Katie Boyle. 'She was very much against taking animals from the wild but there was no way it could be returned. It never grew up very big but it became like a pet. She used to take it down Hampstead High Street on a collar and it slept in her room. When it died she nearly committed suicide.'

Some people are particularly upset when their pet dies because they find it very difficult to make relationships with other people. So on the pet's death they are mourning not only the loss of their pet but their ability to make contact in their lives generally.

'One lady was bereft after the death of a horse,' says Dr Colin Murray Parkes. 'She'd had insecure parenting, she was not close to people, in adult life she'd had an affair with a married man which ended disastrously, as so many do – and the one thing that she could rely on was her horse. When her horse died it was a major bereavement which triggered off severe depression. She was grieving for the loss of all attachment and now the horse had let her down, too.'

And this sad story tells of how a man grieved for the loss of his cat, Woody:

Woody had been the best friend I had ever known. I had always yearned to be loved and Woody had loved in the deepest and purest sense and now she was gone. I sobbed

unashamedly as I walked to my car from the vet's. I placed
the box containing her body on the front seat next to me
and drove off sobbing and weeping like I had never done
before. I stopped to phone my wife but couldn't go home
– it wasn't that I was ashamed to show my grief but I
didn't think I could control it and it would upset my two
boys. I drove down to a local wood and simply sat with
the box next to me and sobbed for an hour.

   This cat used to go for walks with me. And when my
first girlfriend let me down, she comforted me. When I
was bedridden with illness she stayed with me every day.
Some people who saw us together were embarrassed by
our intimacy. It was almost as if we were lovers and some
people found it impossible to accept. I never cared. She
would jump onto my lap, lift her head to my face
demanding kisses and I would kiss her forehead. This
often went on for fifteen minutes before she would settle
contentedly on my lap, purring like a machine. It was the
purest love. There was total unquestioning devotion on
both sides. The understanding between us was almost
psychic. She had been so incredibly sensitive and loyal and
loving and been such a blessing to a sad and lonely man.

                                                      Martin

   Sometimes the loss of a pet will spark off grief for other
bereavements that have not been properly dealt with. This is known
as 'double grief' and happens particularly when, say, one partner is
left widowed but still has the spouse's pet. It's when this pet dies
that the partner suddenly seems to experience all the grief she or he
had been bottling up.
   'I was once referred a woman who was suffering major depression
after the death of her husband's budgie,' says Dr Colin Murray

Parkes. 'And I had another patient who lost several members of her family in the Zeebrugge disaster. She was given some bereavement counselling, did reasonably well – but then came back to me much later suffering from major depression. She had started a stables and then had to sell it, leaving her two horses. They hadn't actually died, but coming back to London, and having to leave her horses behind seemed to have more impact on her than losing her family.'

These cases illustrate how deeply pet bereavement can strike owners:

> My husband died in 1983 and I knew that my dog Brandy was now my sole companion. From that day he slept at the bottom of my bed and I felt safe and not alone. In the first year of my loss my family and friends were full of support, then that suddenly disappeared. Then my eldest son left home and Brandy was my only companion. I often would look at him and dread the day we would have to part company – because now I feel I'm living through the first year of my husband's death but this time with no family or friends to support me. They say he was 'only a dog'. But he was my best friend and so faithful to me; to replace him would be hard, the same as replacing my husband with another man.
>
> Tessa

> My father was heartbroken when his little dog died. It had belonged to his second wife who had died some years before. One Christmas he poured his heart out to me. He felt guilty that he felt more grief over the dog than he had felt for his wife. I told him not to feel guilty, that the dog was all he had left of her and now the dog had gone he felt he had broken all links. He felt so much better after I

explained that.

Peggy

After my husband died, my daughter died in a road
accident. The only thing that kept me going was my dog,
Cindy. And now Cindy has died. I miss her so much. I
keep expecting her to follow me around as she did though
she often fell down with arthritis. One night last summer I
couldn't sleep worrying about a daughter living away and
suffering from a nervous breakdown because of an
accident and alone because of a divorce. I went downstairs
at about 5.30 in the morning, made a cup of tea and sat at
the bottom of my secluded little garden with just the
moonlight for light. Cindy came along and sat by me for
the whole time. What other companion would want to do
that? A neighbour who saw me last week remarked that she
was only a dog. I put her straight. A dog she might be but
she was there loving me when my friends and neighbours
were not.

Margaret

As we've seen, many people use their pets as child substitutes.
'People don't understand how much a pet can give somebody, or the
deep relationship between the owner and pet,' says Averil Jarvis, of
the Cinnamon Trust, a charity devoted to caring for animals after
their owners have died. 'If a person dies you've got all the
paraphernalia of funerals, letters and so on. But losing a pet is
tantamount to losing a child to many people – which is one of the
worst griefs of all.'

And even pets as small as guinea pigs, if they are substitutes for
children, can cause their owners great grief when they die.

Several years ago we adopted two guinea pigs from the nursery where I work. People had grown tired of looking after them so we took them into our home. We had been trying for many years to have children and after sixteen years of marriage had decided we could not undergo any more treatment. Therefore I suppose the guinea pigs filled a gap in our lives. They were regarded as our family. Six months ago Holly became ill – we took her to the vet straight away who treated her with antibiotics. She didn't get any better so we took her to a more sympathetic vet but a week later we were told no more could be done so we rushed her for specialist treatment at Cambridge. Despite all their efforts she died. We went to collect her but on arrival we were shocked to find we had been given the wrong guinea pig and sadly our Holly had been cremated by mistake. The final goodbye is very important to any bereaved person and we had been robbed of ours whilst searching for a way to come to terms with this. But we heard about a pet memorial service and contacted them for a memorial for Holly. We received a very sympathetic reception and had a memorial slate made for Holly. Many people have reacted strangely to our way of dealing with our loss but I don't see that a loving relationship with a pet is any different to that of a person. It felt like we had lost a child and yet I was expected to get over the experience in a matter of days instead of months or even years as with a person.

Joyce

Dr Mary Stewart quotes another touching case. 'When a dog belonging to a childless couple was put down because of persistent fits, the husband went into a state of acute grief. For three weeks he hardly spoke or ate and was very depressed. His wife, in desperation, brought home a pup. Although he had insisted he never wanted another dog, he immediately picked it up, cuddled it, and started to recover. For the next fourteen years the dog was his constant companion. During this time two sons were born. When the old dog finally died, the owner was very sad but showed none of the acute grief symptoms that he had suffered when there had been no children in his life. It seemed again to be a matter of emotional investment. This man may have suffered an intense grief reaction in the first instance, but it would have been considered as a normal reaction if the bereavement had been for a human death. Since the dog had been, to some extent, a child substitute, then his reaction had been appropriate to his emotional investment. His reaction was also proper to the second dog bereavement, where the dog had been a close friend but not a child substitute.'

Dr Mary Stewart has done research into the differences between grief over human bereavement and grief over pet bereavement, and come up with some fascinating results. She concludes that the fact that owners know that pets will die before them seems to make no difference to how much they grieve. She also points out that the owners of pets have to take responsibility for euthanasia, while doctors take responsibility for human euthanasia. Owners of pets are often present at the death of an animal while they're not usually present at the death of humans. And grief generally comes instantly in the case of a pet – not after a period of shock, as with a human bereavement. She also comments that pet owners get very little support and help, and no rituals, often returning on their own to an empty house, compared to those who are humanly bereaved. No one would expect a new widower to continue coming in to work immediately after his wife's death, but it wouldn't be thought appropriate if a bereaved pet owner stayed off work for so much as a day. And finally, she comments that the death of an animal doesn't

seem to have any kind of life-enhancing effect – in other words it
doesn't result in a life review as a human bereavement so often does.

Sometimes I felt as if I was going to burst with tension
inside, sometimes howling at the moon (like my dog!). I
got drunk one night and silently yelled up to the skies:
'You bastards, give me back my dog!' Tears flooded down,
too many to mop up, so that they trickled down the neck.
Sobs wracked my body, wanting so much to touch my
dog. I could still 'see' him – flashbacks, I suppose – out of
the corner of my eye. I could certainly hear him, bumping
down the stairs, a little whine sometimes, a creak on the
bed. I smelt him, too. I used to sniff the places where he
sat and lay to get something of him back.

But I couldn't touch or caress him. I missed that need
we had for me to do this to him and for him to offer up
his body to gain the pleasure he had from it. I remember
his silky ears, his 'paddy paws', his stumpy little tail, the
white silky feeling of his fur. After he had died I did once
'tread' on his foot accidentally as I often did when he was
under the bed, and I apologised for it. He was so
internalised and part of my psyche – I've lost part of what
I am now he is gone. My daily routine, from waking to
bed, involved interaction with my dog. In fact, he initiated
a lot of it and I adapted to his demands, too. So I am still
trying to manage that part of me which was killed when
the injection went into him. I know I was watching myself
die, too. I was also watching that which I had nurtured (I
had him from a puppy and the relationship of love and
training was as a mother with her child), so it was also
watching that which I'd fought to nourish and give life to
and fought so hard to keep as the end approached. And I

was the one who gave the order, because the only other option was suffering – on both sides. So I was angry about the option, quick or slow death, but only death. Boy, was I angry. Why me? Why was I faced with this? I also felt fear, before the death, of having to make the decision, but also some relief also on his death. No more suffering for him or me watching him suffer. No more fear about what lay ahead.

After the death I felt desolated. My son questioned: 'Why are we given life if it's taken like this? What's the point?' I felt some guilt, too. I did let him suffer too long. I felt shocked as well because it crossed my mind to get another dog – it actually took me five years, but there was some relief in knowing that I could accept that life goes on and that I'm not going to be shut up with my grief. After the death we went home and cried and cuddled and said what we felt. We spoke all day and the next about what we were going to miss about him, we didn't want to throw away anything, everything was left exactly as he'd left it, even the sick, urine and faeces he had dropped through that last awful night. We went 'his' walks, tiring ourselves out. I also worked like a maniac at home, cleaning the house except for 'his' places. I feel that the bonding between animals and humans feels very special. Something on a higher level than human love.

Melanie

When she was alive I must have taken more photographs of her than perhaps I did of my own son and husband but she loved every minute of it. Now I no longer have the drive to capture anything on camera since it doesn't include her. It feels as if I lost part of me when she died. I still cry, usually when there isn't anyone around. How long does it take to get over the death of a four-legged friend? Do you know the most heartless thing people say is: 'She was only a dog.' No wonder I prefer animals to people because I love her as much even though she is dead as when she was alive.

Jeannie

Guilt is a common symptom of grief.

I feel bitter the vet didn't do further tests and I wish I had asked him to. I got the impression he thought a dog of thirteen was too old to bother with. When my daughter phoned to say she couldn't wake Lady up I knew she had died. When I got home Lady was still so warm – my baby had died in her sleep. I couldn't go back to work, I suffered from vomiting and diarrhoea. We buried her in the garden – how I hated the earth falling in on her. My son and my husband took two hours to dig the hard, frosty ground. That sight will always be in my mind. When Lady died I had never touched anything dead before. I wanted to cuddle her but her body was stiff – it didn't feel like her. I don't know how I got through that night. I didn't sleep. I had a bright blue flash of colour in my left eye all evening. I told my husband it was just as if it was Lady leaving me. What makes me feel even worse with guilt is the fact that my husband and I had been going through a bad patch in our marriage and there had been a lot of arguments at home, even the night before Lady died. It wasn't a peaceful house at that time. How I wish I could turn the clock back. Some days I feel like dying. I keep thinking our arguments might have made

Lady worse. No one understand how I feel. My husband
can't talk about Lady. He says it is too painful. Although I
have always been loved by my parents, husband and
children, the love that Lady showed me was so special. I
don't think I shall ever experience a bond like that again.
Lady will be with me until I die.'

Laura

According to research, cat owners seem to suffer more than dog
owners when their pets die. And women suffer more than men.

'I certainly see more cat owners than dog owners,' says Suzanne
Thomas. 'I think it's because doggy people are more extrovert, they
take their dogs for walks and all the doggy people around them
grieve with them when they die. Doggy people are more of a
support to one another.'

I still grieve after my lovely cat. I can't eat and have lost
half a stone, I just haven't got any appetite. I think I love
animals more than some people. They have brought me so
much more happiness. When I was ill my cat never left my
bedside, he just sat on my bed looking at me, just leaving
me for a few minutes to go out or eat. He did this for two
weeks. How can you not love this devoted animal and
grieve for him? I know I can't go on like this or I will
make myself ill. I do feel better writing to you because my
friends think I'm not right in my mind.

Eileen

For twenty-three years I have been a semi-invalid, unable
to walk or travel far since I nearly died with a serious virus.
Seven years ago I got this sweet little kitten who was found
in a wood, starving. I nursed him and loved him so much.

He became my best friend, my child and only companion,
particularly as I was unable to go out for months at a time
for weakness. He gave me seven years of the best love ever
known – a love I had never had before, faithful
understanding and perfect manners! I am devastated and
empty and my therapist says I will never be able to replace
him. He gave me a reason for living after years of illness. I
am now severely depressed and cannot stop crying. Gypsy
gave me a greater meaning than I ever found than when I
was able to travel around.

                                                            Sandie

Is pet owning – and pet losing – worth all the pain and suffering?
Yes, says Neil Lyndon, who wrote movingly in *The Times* about his
cat's death:

Two nights before she [his cat] died, she climbed on to my
lap at dinner and would not be removed. She stayed there
for about two hours, fastened in a connection which I
recognised, posthumously, to have been her knowing
farewell. You can't tell me a cat doesn't know when it's got
cancer . . .

The worst thing about keeping animals is not that they
make a monkey out of you while they live, but that they
rip you up when they die. Cats go nobly to their end, but
their owners go to pieces.

This grieving doesn't get any easier to bear with age. The
deaths of our dogs when I was a child did not touch me less
or more than the end of the alley mog which came in my
fortieth year. When my wife's favourite cat was killed on the
road outside our house, we were in mourning for three days.

You may feel that this is no way for a grown-up to

carry on; and I would have to agree. On the other hand, I reckon that you may not fully know yourself as a poor, bare, forked animal if you have never surrendered to the imperial egoism of a cat or recognised that a dog has sussed out every sentimental wrinkle of your character.

Lonely House

No more cat tracks on the floor,
Muddy scratches on the door,
Puffs of hair upon the stairs,
Lacy fretwork on the chairs,

Indentations on my bed,
Markings where she laid her head,
Smudges on the window-pane
Showing where she watched in vain.

Haunts where she is wont to lay
Remind us that she is away.
My house is neater, that is true,
But, oh, how still and empty, too!

Anon

Letters in Wood

Wherever I go she follows me,
My house is her domain;
There isn't a nook or cranny
Where she hasn't staked her claim.
Even though she has left me,
There isn't one tiny place
Where I don't sense her presence
Or remember her cheerful face.

All the years we spent together
Remain buried in my past;
The memories are like diamonds
Forever they will last.
She couldn't speak my language,
She knew that I understood.
Scratch marks on the door,
Are her letters in wood.

Dennis Stevenson

Requiem for Pluto

One large-sized collar hanging by the door
And one lead seldom used, now not needed any more.
One food bowl with Dog on it that you were using yesterday,
A lonely walk without you — but you were with me every
moment of the way
One newly-filled-in grave near the clothesline and the red
May tree,
One heart very badly broken — and that belongs to me.

Anon

Chapter 3

⌘

When a Child's Pet Dies

Most people's first experience of bereavement comes from the death of a pet when they were young. They may never have quite understood what 'dead' actually means – but now they see something dead for the first time.

When asked about their first experience of bereavement, nearly all the medical students training on one course said that their only experience of bereavement to date was with pets – hamsters, cats or dogs.

Obviously some children shrug off the death of a pet, often quite relieved they don't have to look after it any more – but adults often misjudge the importance of a pet to a child. These quotes came from a study of children and pets and show us how close the connection can be between children and their animals: 'I save up to buy things for it,' 'I like teaching it tricks,' 'It's something of my own to look after,' 'He's always there – gets me up in the mornings, sees me on to the school bus, and he's there when I get home, and goes to bed with me,' 'When I'm sad it always is able to cheer me up,' 'He makes me happy when I am sad and is company when I'm lonely,' 'He guards the house and I feel safer when he's around,' 'He's my friend, my pal, one of the family,' 'He cuddles into me, loves having his tummy rubbed,' 'He's pretty and fluffy,' 'I love taking it to the park,' 'It's fun to watching him jumping around,' 'My dad and I go hunting with him and people stop to stroke him.'

Small wonder that when their pets die children can feel devastated: 'I felt lonely and began to cry . . .' 'I cried and cried and cried until I could cry no more, I didn't believe it. I didn't know where I was,' 'I cried all morning at school,' 'He was the only one who understood when I was upset,' 'I could tell him all my troubles and he never got angry with me,' 'He was the only thing I could count on when my parents split up,' 'When I was ill and had to stay in bed she was with me all the time.' Children may feel particularly upset if someone close to them has died recently. Their grief, which may seem inappropriate over the death of, say, a stick insect, may really be for the friend or relative who has just died.

It is terribly important to let children express their feelings – to listen to them and answer all their questions as honestly as you can, and not to hold back if you, too, feel grief. It's also important to let them see the body, if they want to see it, and involve them in the whole process – if, of course, they want to be involved.

If a child is two or three years old, they may not really have an idea of what death is about. They simply think the animal has gone to sleep – but it's important not to associate the word 'sleep' with the word 'death'. Otherwise they may be terrified of falling asleep, worrying that they may not wake up in the morning. It's also important not to lie and say that a dead animal has 'gone missing'. Often it's far worse for a child to imagine a pet is lost and pining for its owner than knowing that it is dead and at peace.

Four to six year olds often imagine that their animals live on in some way – either underground where they're buried, or in some kind of 'heaven'. Some children are very anxious that the pet's death was their fault, and it's worth reassuring them that they played no part in it. They also may start worrying that just because a pet dies, they – or members of their family – are going to die, too. Again, reassurance should be offered that nothing like that is likely to happen at all.

In order to answer the question 'Where does it go when it dies?' you can talk of heaven if that is what you believe, or just say that it has joined all the other dead people and pets to make a new life.

Don't think that one session of explanation and reassurance will do. During the time following a pet's death, it's worth referring to the event at least a couple of times a day, so that any anxieties a child might have produced about it can be aired. It's no bad thing to encourage the child to draw pictures of their dead pet, or, perhaps, create a little memory book. Remember that children, after the death of a pet, may well find their sleep is disturbed or they wet the bed or behave in a more withdrawn, angry or obstreperous way.

Don't throw away the pet's toys and collar without consulting the child. He or she will feel utterly powerless in the face of a death, so it's important to give them as much say in the whole process afterwards as possible. Maybe they'd prefer it if, rather than throwing the toys and so on away, you were to give them to an animal rescue centre. If you're going to bury the animal's body in the garden, for instance, let them dig part of the grave. Or they could write a poem to bury with the body. It's worth letting them choose the bulbs to plant on the grave, or bury a picture with the body. And don't get upset if a child switches from being grief stricken to showing a macabre interest in the whole process. 'Why doesn't its eyes shut?' they may ask. Or: 'Can we dig it up tomorrow and look at it?'

After nine years old, children tend to feel grief in the same way as adults, but remember that even if a child appears not to mind about an animal dying, he or she may well be suffering underneath.

Whatever you do, don't try to substitute another pet without telling them. Children will always notice the difference. I remember when once I had a hamster from my son's school to stay over half term. It got eaten by our cat. I tried to find a lookalike but in the end I had to confess and just put another hamster in its place. The teacher assured me that no one in the class were very upset about it.

'I was about eleven when my mice died,' says Jenny, 13:

> They'd just sort of always been there and it was a shock when they just weren't. I built a Lego house for them with fleecy stuff inside it for them. It became a chore looking after them but I hadn't realised how upset I'd be when they did die.
>
> They were my first pets and I felt very protective of them. We had mice in the house, so on the one hand we were killing them and the thought of our domestic mice ever getting out and eating the poisonous food was awful. It was very odd.
>
> I think William died from old age. My mum told me that he had died when I got back from school. At first I couldn't understand what she meant, then she showed me, and he was just lying there and the other mouse was just very quiet next to him, normally always chattering away by the food bowl and he seemed sad.
>
> We waited till my dad came home and then we took the body out and put him in a king-size box of matches and put a doily and pot-pourri in it, and dug a little grave in the back garden and planted Sweet Williams on top. It was so sad. We had to dig deep to get him down because I

was terrified cats would get him. Friends at school were
very understanding because they'd had hamsters who'd
died and they were nice. Weeks later I'd sometimes
wonder what his skeleton would look like in the earth.
The Sweet Williams never grew.

If God Had Wanted a Gerbil

If God had wanted a gerbil
He should have saved up like me
And gone to the pet shop and bought one
That's doing things properly.

If God had wanted a gerbil
Then I think it awfully mean
To have made me drop mine and kill it
When I fed it and kept it so clean.

If God had wanted a gerbil
He should have taken its cage and straw
No, I won't have another gerbil
Just in case God wants some more.

Anon

Chapter 4

Putting a Pet to Sleep

'I have decided about Queenie. She is to have her quietus
tomorrow, if the vet can manage. Now I have taken the
decision I feel quite calm; it will be a great relief not to have
to see her in her present state any more. She has dwindled
away and is as gaunt as Don Quixote; when I carried her on
to the terrace this morning and watched her try to defecate
and collapsing, I realised with absolute conviction (the thing
I have hitherto lacked) that the end of the journey had
come. The sense of pity has come; it is at last utterly clear
that life is a humiliation and a burden to her. The relief of
no longer having to fight this so sad, so disappointing losing
battle will be greater than the grief, I hope.'

J.R. Ackerley writing to James Kirkup about his Alsatian.

28 October 1961

My worst experience of putting a pet to sleep came when
our neighbours acquired a little white and ginger kitten.
It was always coming through our cat door and asking
for food – but though I gave it the occasional saucer of milk I

definitely did not want a third cat. Nor, indeed, did my other two cats. Gradually this little chap's visits became more frequent. And although he was obviously fed by the neighbours, something was seriously wrong. His miaows became more pitiful; when he opened his mouth he would give a painful howl at the same time – and I noticed the inside of his mouth had turned a dreadful yellow colour.

After a few days of this (and a few hints about vets to the neighbours which were ignored), I took my courage into my hands, bundled the poor creature into my cat basket, and took him on a surreptitious visit to a local vet.

The moment the vet set eyes on the cat he started yelling at me. 'How dare you let a cat get into this condition!' he shouted. 'People like you are not fit to own animals! This poor cat is in the most terrible pain and is terminally ill! I shall have to put him down at once! You have treated this animal cruelly by not bringing him for treatment earlier . . .' and so on.

I feebly explained it was not my cat, that I had kidnapped him, that I couldn't possibly have him put down since he wasn't my property. And, feeling like a sadist, I bundled him back into the basket and took him to the door. The vet and his assistant looked after me, balefully. I paused. No, I couldn't let him suffer any longer. I might be doing wrong in law, my neighbours might never speak to me again, but morally I could not let this animal live in pain. I took the basket back to the table, handed it over to the vet, told him to put the poor chap out of his misery, paid the bill and left.

This episode brought out more feelings of guilt than I've ever had before when having an animal put down. I felt terribly guilty I hadn't taken it to the vet earlier; I also felt terribly guilty I had allowed it to be put down since it wasn't mine. I felt guilty about killing my neighbour's cat – they were nice people, after all. I felt terrified about what they might do to me if they found out. I also felt dreadful that this little creature had had such a short, unhappy and painful life and that I had not responded with more care – the harsh words of the vet rang in my ears. I tossed and turned all night with anxiety before I eventually wrote a tortured letter to my neighbours explaining what I had done. And after spending about three months crawling out of my house on hands and knees so they wouldn't see me over the wall, one finally popped his head over and said: 'Oh, thank you for sorting the cat out, by the way! That was very kind of you!'

Euthanasia means 'gentle and easy death'. Many vets dislike the phrase 'putting a pet to sleep' and prefer to use the phrase 'bringing your pet's life to an end'. Personally, it doesn't really matter to me which phrase they use – we all know what they mean. What euthanasia is *not*, however, is mere 'killing', at least not if, like me, you regard that word as having aggressive and murderous overtones.

One vet described his dilemma: 'We do it so frequently – put animals down – that we probably forget it's the most important thing we do for that animal or that owner,' he says. 'For that reason alone the whole procedure, the transition from life to death, should be as smooth as possible for both the pet and the owner.

'What we must remember is that when we put pets to sleep who cannot live normal lives we're doing the kindest thing for an animal that any human being can do. We have the ability and the right to put him to sleep.

'The use of consent forms is essential because there can be misunderstandings and there can be one member of a family bringing the cat or dog in without the other knowing. But it all must be done tactfully and kindly.

'The owner should always be offered the choice of whether to be present at the euthanasia or not and I tend to persuade them to stay because it is a procedure which is terribly smooth and terribly peaceful and the old dog or cat is usually in some distress. To see the transition from life to peaceful death is an eye-opener for a client.

'Owners should always be offered a few minutes on their own with the body – the men usually show more grief than the ladies amazingly. Afterwards, in my practice, I usually then re-enter and we wrap the pet in a blanket. But if they're taking the pet away with them then it's easy to say to them, kindly: "Look, I'm afraid the bladder and bowels do relax after death and it's likely the urine will soak into your car, so would you like us to put some polythene around him?"

'If the pet is being cremated, a vet should always ask about the collar and lead – does the client want it cremated with the pet? If they say they don't mind, it's worth keeping because sometimes the client will ring up asking for it back later.'

In more recent years many vets have offered to put pets to sleep at home. John Bower says: 'One has to balance the stress of waiting for the vet to come to the home with the fact that when it happens at home the owner is invariably happy to hold their animal in its own surroundings which is probably nicer for all concerned.' But other vets disagree. They say it is best for owners, if they bring sick animals in, to perform the euthanasia there and then in order not to prolong the agony and torment.

This is how Cheryl described the euthanasia of two different pets. You can see which venue she preferred:

> People constantly badgered me to have my dog put down, but he didn't suffer and still looked very healthy despite being terminally ill. With all good intent, people thoroughly annoyed me by stating this is better for animals, as they can be put out of their misery, while humans have to suffer. Yet when actually faced with euthanasia for a dear and much-loved member of the

family, thoughts get very confused. What right had I to do this to him? He trusted me completely and there I was planning to kill him! He had as much right to life as anyone and after we had had him put to sleep in the surgery I felt like a murderer. We vowed we would never do such a thing to a dog again. It was terrible. After his death I wanted to tell everyone we knew. I must have bored the pants off people by my long and lengthy description of the death in every gory detail. We couldn't believe it, so I suppose we had to convince ourselves of the fact that he'd gone by telling everyone what a dreadful experience it had been. What shocked us both was, the day after he died, and we'd buried him in the garden, we both wanted to dig him up again! We didn't of course, but the feeling was very strong.

But with their next dog it was a different story:

I called the vet, gave her the sedatives, and we strolled out to the garden together and sat on the grass. My husband came home, my youngest daughter was present, and we all quietly savoured those last moments with her. She lay peacefully asleep across my legs when the vet arrived. She was unaware of his presence. He, too, sat quietly with us for at least fifteen minutes before he gently gave her the injection. As it was going in I told her we were going for a walk in her favourite woods. I spoke to her in her ear, holding her close, till she left us. We buried her close to our other dog in our garden. The vet stayed for another half an hour, joining in our grief. The next day he wrote me a letter to say it was quite the nicest, most peaceful euthanasia he had ever attended.

The role of the vet during euthanasia is often crucial to how a person reacts later. Aine Wellard, a pet bereavement counsellor, wrote: 'In a crisis situation when the client is in a state of heightened awareness, almost everything the veterinary surgeon says and does has a greater significance than would normally be the case. If the situation is handled well, the veterinary surgeon is in a position to facilitate a healthy grief response by helping to prevent anger and alleviate guilt which, in turn, decreases the client's sense of isolation and helplessness . . . The veterinary surgeon, almost by default, determines how a person reacts to the loss of his or her pet.'

> I had to put my dog to sleep on the vet's advice – he was a collie of fourteen. The vet asked if I would agree and I can't think where the words came from. I said: 'Okay, if you think it's best,' and within minutes the vet was saying: 'He is gone.' The vet and the assistant were very good, assuring me they would take care of the cremation and letting me go out of the back door to save my embarrassment. You see I am not a female or young, I am a fully grown, strapping, fourteen-stone man, retired ex-training officer, forty years in the mining industry. I've made many hard decisions without batting an eyelid. But even as I write this I am crying and my head aches with trying to hold the tears back. Sometimes I find myself stepping over him or sometimes open the door to let him in or I sometimes see his profile standing in the garden even though he's gone. My wife, my dog and I retired to live here and enjoy walking along the sands and prom meeting many people on holiday with their dogs. But as many friends with dogs are arriving for the season I find myself avoiding them as I can't talk about Harvey. When I meet any of them, their first comment is: 'Where's your dog?' and it sets me off in tears.

Hugh

Unfortunately vets barely have any training at all in how to deal with clients during euthanasia. If they're lucky they'll have an afternoon's lecture, but that's usually about it. One survey showed that 96 per cent of vets said they had no formal training at all in how to explain to a client that their pet is terminally or critically ill.

'I've gone round lots of vets' surgeries taking to vets and their nurses about what happens when someone loses an animal,' says Suzanne Thomas. 'They are often very distressed to see people's very raw pain. Someone's there in floods of tears and wants to talk and they don't know what to do. Should they drag them away from the animal or not? Should they talk or leave them alone? Maybe it's none of my business, they think – or do their clients want a shoulder to cry on? They don't know.'

Cathy Davis, a veterinary nurse, says: 'When you come across animals who have to be put to sleep you're left to deal with it on your own. Veterinary nurses are expected to simply accept it, without any training. No one ever says to you: "This may not look very nice but this is what we're going to do." Invariably at her first euthanasia the nurse bursts into tears. Of course eventually you get philosophical about it mostly and you learn that the best thing to do is to put an animal to sleep *properly*. That's the only consolation you've got when you're putting it to sleep – you feel, even with a stray which no one wants: "Well, at least no one's going to dump you on a motorway now."'

These days a little more attention is being paid to training vets in this difficult area – particularly at the Veterinary School at Glasgow University where Dr Mary Stewart took a particular interest in the subject. 'I did quite a lot of work on human/animal relationships and mentioned what shape bereavement takes. In the final year we had a couple of hours with small group sessions where we presented students with a couple of problem areas to do with euthanasia and owner grief, and got them to discuss them.

'What a vet really fears is that he won't do a good job, that they won't get the injection into the vein. It's so important that everything is right and the animal isn't struggling and screaming when they go out.

'Once they're not so worried about that, then vets are more inclined to consider the owners. They are confused about what they should do and how to comfort people. Some are intuitively wonderful, but some need a little prodding to make them much more aware.

'It is very distressing for vets personally when they've known the animal for a long time, and have to acknowledge that the animal hasn't responded to treatment. But the worst is when the owner is very dependent on the dog or perhaps has to go into sheltered housing, but can't take his perfectly fit old friend with him. The vet's heart is breaking for both the client and the pet who he has to put down.

'The other moment when it is very hard for vets is when people are nonchalant about their animal's life, and ask for it to be put down because it's shedding hairs over the house, or the wife says: "The dog or me." Putting down a healthy animal for no good reason is terrible.'

As a vet says: 'Your elderly pet is no different from grandma or grandpa and their requirements are just the same. If the dog is happy and free of pain and can plod around the house and the garden, enjoys its food and sleeps at night and isn't anti-social by being incontinent, or vomiting, then that's fine. It's amazing the number of people who feel that because the dog can't do any exercise then it ought to be put to sleep. But you wouldn't haul grannie round the block, would you?'

In a chapter in his contribution to the book *Euthanasia and the Companion Animal*, Bernard E. Rollin writes: 'For veterinarians in pet practice, the demand that they kill healthy animals for the convenience of their owners is a constant source of stress . . . People want animals killed for the most appalling reasons: they have no use for a litter of puppies and only wanted their children to witness "the miracle of birth"; they have undergone psychoanalysis and are no longer "poodle persons" but "Doberman persons"; they are moving and don't want the difficulty of finding a place that takes pets; they are going on vacation and don't wish to spend the kennel fee since it is cheaper to get a new dog at the pound; the animal no longer matches their colour scheme; the dog barks, urinates, chews, chases children, digs up the yard, is too old to jog with them, and so on.' All this, he argues, puts tremendous stress on vets who only went into practice to help and nurture animals in the first place.

One of the worst results of the Dangerous Dogs Act, 1991, is, according to Roger Mugford of the Animal Behaviour Centre, the way that so-called dangerous animals are seized often in the early hours and taken off to await judgement and appeals. In a report from the Society for Companion Animal Studies he writes: 'A succession of legal and bureaucratic obstacles then deny owners access to their dogs, creating a catastrophic anxiety that their pet may be suffering or indeed have been killed by the authorities. These dogs are the modern day "disappeared ones", with owners suffering the same psychological traumas as those documented for Argentine mothers in the 1970s . . . The bodies of dogs which are killed by this system are generally not returned to their owners, creating more scope for real or imagined fears about their pet's suffering. Such owners report repeated nightmares about their pets and suffer an uncontrollable grief that they and a veterinarian of their choice could not give it a kind, final goodbye. Grief turns to helpless depression in some victims of this legislation; in others it creates rage against a system which is plainly absurd.'

Which brings us to the other problem that vets have to contend with – clients' anger. Since one of the so-called 'stages' of grief is often rage, the vets are natural butts of owners' fury at the fact their pet has died or been put down. Apparently the most common complaint received by the Royal College of Veterinary Surgeons about its members is that of insensitivity – most frequently in relation to the euthanasia of pets.

But that's just the down side. One vet wrote saying that one of the most satisfying things that happened to him was getting notes from clients thanking him for the way he had coped with their animals' death.

When her guide dog had to be put down, Aine Wellard wrote: 'I had not realised that death could be so peaceful and found the whole new experience strangely therapeutic. I say strangely because I would not have believed that it was possible to take a decision to kill a dog who had meant so much to me, and not have any feelings of guilt or remorse. Theoretically it should have been a harrowing experience. After all, I wasn't just losing a dog, I was saying goodbye to part of my life. I felt sad; I felt very, very sad, but I knew the right decision had been taken and I had no regrets. My peace of mind and clear conscience was all due to the way in which the vet had handled the events of that day.'

And another woman wrote to a veterinary journal simply 'to place on record my very sincere thanks for the kindness and sympathy shown to me by a vet during the recent death of my cat. How wonderful it would be if the medical profession were as courteous, caring and compassionate, instead of being irascible, unhelpful and condescending towards their patients. They could well learn valuable lessons from the veterinary fraternity.'

If you get your pet put down you almost invariably feel guilty – even though on another level you probably know that you deserve a pat on the back. Some people say, 'Maybe we should have had him put down sooner, but we couldn't bear to part with him'; others say, 'Maybe we should have waited longer, given him a little while . . .';

or 'If only I had stayed with him when he was dying . . .'; or 'If only we had asked the vet to come to the house.'

It is now just over a year since his death and I do feel better although sometimes I long to put my arms around him and comfort him; also I feel an enormous sense of guilt due to the stress I often felt when he was with us; I sometimes lost my temper with him. Immediately after his death I started to imagine awful things like the vet hadn't given him a large enough dose of anaesthetic to kill him and I keep wondering if we shouldn't have tried something like homeopathy.

June

My biggest regret was that I didn't have him cremated or bring him home to bury in the garden. I held him, telling him I loved him and always would, when the vet put that needle in his leg. The vet said it was cruel to him to keep him alive any longer. I know I did the right thing but it leaves a great hole in your heart. Shep was my life. I have photos of him around my house. He's even on a music tape, barking.

Vicky

When Cindy was fourteen years old she got rheumatism in her legs and she could hardly stand. We had to make the decision to have her put to sleep. That was the worst day of my life. I felt like a murderer. I had never seen my husband break down and cry before. I felt as if I had lost not only my friend but a child. I couldn't get over the grief and I nearly had a breakdown. I was off work for three months and on tranquillisers for nearly a year.

Judy

And finally, this tragic story from a woman in Ireland:

> Please help me before I crack up. A month ago I had our
> dog put down and I haven't stopped crying since. I loved
> him so much and I feel as if I betrayed him. The reason he
> was put down was because he was snappy at the child's
> face sometimes and given the chance, he would grab at
> everyone's heels, even ours. People kept telling me he was
> going to be very cross when he grew up. He was only seven
> months. I was influenced by others and I can't forgive
> myself for doing it. If only I could turn back the clock. It
> might not seem like a problem to you, but it feels like a
> major crime to me.

If you feel guilty, my own suggestion is to sit down and talk to
your pet, wherever he is now. Ask him if you did the right thing.
Almost certainly he will be barking or purring excitedly to show
you that it was the kindest thing you could possibly have done for
him. You either put him out of his pain, or in the case of the last
lady, you prevented him doing something which, through no fault
of his own, he could not have borne to have done were he able to
think – injuring a child. In most cases, putting a pet down is
probably not just the kindest thing you ever do for your pet, and the
most unselfish – but quite probably it would be very wrong, if the
vet recommends it, *not* to agree to do it.

Fidelity

There's a certain kind of friendship
That is very difficult to beat.
And very rare to find
In the people that you meet:
Yet every dog that ever lived
Has this gift to bestow —
A loyal, firm devotion
As so many of us know.
Though people judge you by your looks,
Your cash, your job, your car,
A dog is so much wiser -
He accepts you as you are.
You can be a saint or sinner
Down-and-out or millionaire,
He'll not ask to see your pedigree
As long as you are there.
While those around are planning
All their trips to Greece and Spain,
With him you'll find adventure
In a romp along the lane.
His days are full of pleasure
Yet his needs are very few,
A pat, a dish, a cushion,
A ball to fetch for you.
If others seem to shun you
Maybe think you're just a bore,
He lets you keep on talking,
Though he's heard it all before,
As he settles close beside you
With his head upon your knee,

For there's no place in all the world
Where he would rather be.
When many may be missing
In your hour of need and strife
There's one who's always ready
To defend you with his life.
No matter whether right or wrong,
He'll never criticise,
But shows his trusting confidence
In clear, adoring eyes.
And when his life is ending
From the signs that you can tell
That joy has turned to misery
And he never will get well
And the tail that wagged in ecstasy
To greet you at the door,
Is hanging low, and honest eyes
Are sad, and shine no more,
It will break your heart to do it
For you know you'll miss him so
But when active life is over
Then it's kinder to let go.
Just to make his ending easy
Is the last thing you can give
And let him die with dignity
The way you let him live.

Doris Tewster

Old Dog

Yes, they have left him
No, there's nought to do
Save let him out of life the gentle way
For wear of body tissues past repair
Is that hard price so many years must pay.

Yes, I have known him since he was a pup
I vaccinated him long years ago
And treated him a score of times since then —
Somehow it's fitting I should let him go.

He trusts me and holds up a paw, unasked:
'One needle more, old friend — the best and last.'
Thus to put off the weariness of pain —
Slip soft from sleep to silence, suffering past.

Peter Horridge

If It Should Be

If it should be I grow frail and weak,
And pain should wake me from my sleep,
Then you must do what must be done,
For this last battle can't be won.
You will be sad, I understand,
Don't let your grief then stay your hand,
For this day more than all the rest,
Your love and friendship stand the test.
We've had so many happy years,
What is to come will hold no fears,
You'll not want me to suffer, so,
When the time comes, please let me go.
I know in time you too will see,
It is kindness you do me,
Although my tail its last has waved,
From pain and suffering I've been saved.
Do not grieve that it should be you,
Who has to decide this thing to do
We've been so close, we two, these years,
Don't let your heart hold any tears.

Anon

We'll Walk Together Once More

With a lump in my throat, I hung up my coat,
And replaced your old lead in the drawer.
Sat down in the chair, ran a hand through my hair
As I realised you'd be there no more.

The vet said: 'It's old age — it's the end of the page
It's something we cannot ignore.'
It was ended I knew and I cried then as you
Went alone through that great final door.

When we entered the vet's, others sat with their pets,
Watched us walk side by side, 'cross the floor.
Then I came out alone and started back home —
They all knew I should see you no more.

When I think of the years, the laughter, the tears,
All our walks over meadow and tor,
Of your sparkling brown eyes, I just can't realise
That I shall look in them no more.

But there will come a time when I'm well past my prime,
You'll be waiting my friend
As I get to the end
And we'll walk together once more.

Betty Kirk

Euthanasia

Poor, gentle, noble animal, your pain
Which vexed you sore and long, is over now.
The neat, small, red-edged hole in silver brow
I try in vain to hide with silver mane.

When skill and science fail, there does remain
One last resort which mercy will allow
And did with love the leaden ball endow
Which but one minute past destroyed your brain.

Your dark, wise eyes, now dull and glazed in death,
Look now, perhaps, upon a fairer land;
Your spirit, freed, flies thankful for its rest.
And should such pain precede my final breath
To ease my way will any kindly hand
Rise up and pre-empt God at my request?

                              Martin W.M. Prentice MRCVS

Chapter 5

∞∞∞

Burial or Cremation?

'Near this spot are deposited the remains of one who
possessed Beauty without Vanity, Strength without
Insolence, Courage without Ferocity, and all the Virtues
of Man, without his vices. This Praise, which would be
unmeaning Flattery if inscribed over human ashes, is but a
just tribute to the Memory of Boatswain, a dog.'
Inscribed by Byron on his dog's headstone

People bury their pets and mark the spot so that their
memories live on. All that remains of the love they had for
the animal may be only a small headstone or a little box of
dusty ashes, but whenever they look at it they will remember happy
shared memories. Indeed, sometimes gravestones of hundreds of
years ago can remind us of the love that our ancestors had for their
pets.

If you happen to walk in London along the Bayswater Road by
Hyde Park, past Victoria Lodge, turn your head to peer through the
railings, and you will see an extraordinary sight. Crowded together
and looking like a goblins' war cemetery are three hundred tiny

marble gravestones. This is the Hyde Park Pet Cemetery, which was open between 1880 and 1915 for the burial of pet dogs who loved the park.

Apart from a few small cemeteries in grand country houses, where the pets of the household were buried, there have been very few pet cemeteries until recently. The Hyde Park Pet Cemetery was an exception. And it was almost entirely organised by one man, the lodgekeeper, Mr Windbridge.

According to the *Strand Magazine* of the period, he was a man of a 'kindly, benevolent countenance, who sported a red waistcoat and gold-laced hat' and it was he who usually performed the burial ceremony. 'But only rarely in the presence of the bereaved owners of the lamented pet, who are mostly too much overcome with grief to be able to face this last cruel parting. The dogs are mostly sewn up in canvas bags and are thus committed to their last resting place. In a few instances only have neatly polished deal coffins been used.'

Through these charming memorials, the memories of the dogs linger on; memories of little Centi, Topper – and Smut. 'How suggestive is the name of "Smut", dear little Smut! We can almost see him standing before us. Smut must have been a pug dog – we are positive that he was a pug – a pug with a delicious black nose, which looked as though he had popped his head into the coal-scuttle, and with large, affectionate eyes, made interesting by the enormous dark circles under them, which gave him the air of a Spanish beauty. We feel certain that Smut must have been the perfection of languid and sentimental exquisiteness, if it had not been for a certain latent roguishness about the corners of his eyes during five o'clock tea time, and a hopelessly vulgar habit of hanging out just half an inch of his tongue.'

As for Cherry, he was the pet of the children of Mr and Mrs J. Lewis Barned who were frequenters of the park. A Maltese terrier, graceful, elegant and dandified, 'he was an accomplished dog of the world and delighted in giving drawing room entertainments. Dressing up as a little soldier in a little uniform coat, a helmet and a musket, he was an inimitable sentinel. But as a sick baby carefully tucked up in a perambulator, he always "brought down the house."' In the mornings it was Cherry's invariable custom to fetch his mistress's letters and carry them up into her room. When the door was locked Cherry could not get in so he would gently push them underneath the door. 'So intelligent and amiable a dog assuredly deserved a Christian burial.'

In a report from the Society for Companion Animal Studies, Nick Rickets of the Association of Private Pet Cemeteries and Crematoria wrote: 'The media tend to treat pet cemeteries and crematoria as rather freaky and imply there is something strange about those who use their services. I feel dreadfully sad for all those pet owners who would like to use the facilities of pet cemeteries and crematoria but fear the ridicule of family and friends. We in the business are heartily sick of tales of the "slick, glitzy performances" operating in America and totally alien to us Brits. Over here, in keeping with our reserve, we aim to undertake a high standard of service, and to conduct our operations with sympathy, undertanding and integrity.'

Certainly, today there are many more pet cemeteries around and many more people are taking advantage of making a permanent memorial to their pets.

Maggie Annable runs the Rossendale Pet Cemetery and Crematorium which started 26 years ago. It boasts 1,500 graves and is the biggest pet cemetery in England.

'I never thought I'd be doing a job like this,' she says. 'Even though I used to bury ladybirds in a matchbox when I was a little girl. Certainly every time I mention what I do, everyone goes quiet. It started off with the original farmer of the land running over his dog with a tractor by mistake and putting up a headstone, and then someone asked if they could also bury their animal there.

'We get so many people who apologise to us when they get upset, saying: "You must think I'm stupid." But of course they're not.

'Sometimes they want a favourite cuddly toy buried with the dog, we've had Hindus who've covered the graves with candles and food — and we also have quite a few Jewish pet owners come here, who don't like cremation.

'One lady who breeds budgies has got a bird-bath and every time a budgie dies she brings it up and buries it at the foot of it. She comes about once a year. We have parrots, a lioness, a goldfish, hamsters in tiny coffins and rabbits. One man had to be pulled away from the crematorium when he leant to kiss his Irish wolfhound goodbye and it was already lit.

'Some come up every week to put flowers on the grave, a lot come up at the anniversary of the death and many order a wreath at Christmas. It's true that quite a few owners are childless but often the whole family will come. We have one old couple who've been coming up every year for ten years.'

Mrs Flemens has a pet cemetery near Nuneaton, which started when a dog at their boarding kennels died. Now they have created a beautiful garden 'with a budgie under a rose tree and the odd rabbit or two as well as cats and dogs of course. Many of our clients prefer to bury their pets in their baskets or soft plush beds, and lower them into the ground like that. Then they throw flowers in. Some people tell me they want their own ashes to go into their pet's grave when they die, which is a lovely idea.

'Sad? Yes, but you do get used to it and seem to know what to say when the time comes. But I feel most people have no idea how some pet owners can suffer. I've seen some people hold up better when a member of the family dies.'

After he had been put to sleep in our garden, Gus was picked up by some lovely people who have a pet cemetery with three hundred graves in it. They took Gus's body and we followed them home to see the place that Gus would be in. It was beautiful. They live on the side of a valley overlooking lovely countryside, they are such nice people and they made what was an awful day a little easier for mum and I. They made us tea and showed us where Gus would be buried. It was nothing pretentious, just like a garden really. Some of the graves have small headstones with simple messages to much-loved pets. There are heathers planted around. We feel a little better that Gus is in such a wonderful place but his loss is like that of anyone or thing that passes away. It may sound stupid to some when there is so much horror in this world, to get so upset about a dog. But like so many before him, Gus was part of a family, and a member of that family who shared in everything they did. He gave us so much and in my book that affords a little payback.

Lori

In the United States, pet cemeteries are quite commonplace – and, like all things American, the ceremonies, tombs and headstones can be quite over the top. But Americans *do* take pet death seriously. When it was discovered that a cemetery had conned a couple out of their money, the law came down on the wrongdoers like a ton of bricks.

'A dead dog's owners have been awarded £600,000 damages because pet cemetery owners tricked them over its burial,' reported the *Daily Mail*. 'Joyce Walp and Michael Bachmann were awarded the cash for stress and trauma after discovering their beloved sheepdog Ruffian was not buried in a grave for which they paid £600. The couple wanted Ruffian to rest in peace with his favourite toys, pink blanket and white collar in a hillside plot in the Long Island Pet Cemetery.

'They made weekly trips to put flowers beneath the tombstone,' a New York court heard. But when they heard that the cemetery owners had been arrested for improperly disposing of pets' bodies they dug up the grave and found another dog.

'Ruffian was one of the hundreds of pets "lost" in the scandal which emerged after authorities discovered a mass grave.

'Mr Bachmann, who lost 60lb and suffers recurring nightmares, said: "I still don't know where my dog is." Judge Stuart Ain awarded them the damages "to prevent similar outrageous conduct."

'Cemetery owners Samuel Strauss, 71, and his son, Allan, 36, have closed the cemetery and are out on bail after receiving 41-month and 63-month jail sentences and fines totalling £50,000.'

Some people bury their pets at home in the garden. It is important to dig a hole deep enough to prevent the animal being dug up by other animals – and not to bury it in a plastic bag since gases can build up and the decaying process is held up.

> After a long illness, never having been really well, I made a
> cardboard box for you and lined it with your blue blanket.
> I could not stay with you when the vet came but sat
> outside in the car. Your dad went up the garden to dig
> your grave and they laid one of your toys between your
> paws. When I saw the vet's car go I came indoors. Your
> dad was attempting to tie up your little cardboard coffin
> but three times he broke down and sobbed before he could
> bring himself to do it. I had never seen him cry before in
> all of our thirty-six years together. Oh, Nick, the
> heartache, it's just three months now since you went and I
> have cried every single day and it doesn't get any better!
>
> Cynthia

The Cambridge Pet Crematorium, set in six acres of garden, is the largest in Europe. A large number of pets are cremated communally but each week 700 pets are cremated individually.

'We cremate horses, snakes, rats, rodents – we've done a crocodile, a chimpanzee and I even had a lady who wanted her chicken individually cremated!' says Clive Jackman, who started it in 1979 with his son-in-law, the current managing director. 'I was sure it was a joke but sure enough she came the next day with her chicken and we did it for her.'

Clive Jackman is very keen on people attending their pets' cremations. 'Oh yes, we try to encourage it. They'll come in here with their dog or cat in their car and we'll take care of them, while their pet is being cremated. We used to give them a cup of tea or whatever, but people expect more these days so we've built a lovely new suite of rooms where they can say goodbye to their pet. Some like to say a prayer or read a poem and maybe give them a last pat on the head.

'It's very similar to a human cremation in a sense because everything is set in place and is private for grieving. They can cry which I think is good for them anyway. After all, they wouldn't be here if they didn't want to cry. We have boxes of tissues for them en route. And there is always a counsellor available if they want to see one.'

After it's over, the bereaved owners are led into a small lounge where they wait to receive the ashes and they can choose a casket or browse through Clive Jackman's volumes of remembrance which include letters and photos from hundreds and hundreds of happy clients.

Clive Jackman's biggest fear is that people might worry that they aren't getting the ashes of their pet. That's why he and his son-in-law have made sure there is no room for any slip up between the pet being removed from the viewing room by the member of staff once the family has left the room, and the packaging and presentation of the ashes to them.

'I had one client who didn't want to see anything, but by the look on his face I just knew that he was worried about the ashes. So after the cremation I said: "When did the dog break his leg?" And he said: "How did you know?" So in his hand I put the stainless steel plate I'd found on the tray, with all the little screws, and you could see a weight lift from his shoulders and a big grin of relief came over his face.

'I always badger them to come. I say: "How long did you have your dog?" And they say ten years or whatever. And I say: "And you can't spend three quarters of an hour with him at the end, why not? You won't see anything that will upset you at all." Then they usually cave in. And they're always pleased they came.'

What does upset Clive Jackman is when people don't take a bereaved pet owner's grief seriously. 'The tide is turning, especially with so many women becoming vets. Some vets from the old school, who I've known in the past have thought, well, if they're dead, end of story. But that's where they make their mistake. The story goes on for the person who's lost the pet. It goes on, until they can safely dispose of that body with a bit of dignity in the way that they want and then go home and gradually get over, in time, their bereavement.'

We couldn't bear to have our dogs flung on a rubbish dump so we had them cremated. Last Wednesday we went to the pets' cremation centre where they had been taken – and their ashes were scattered over a small, lovely flower garden. The people who own this business are so caring and kind. We sat on a seat by the garden and they brought us tea and talked of various animals and about their business. We went into the reception office and there were

little crosses and urns you could put on the graves. There
was a baby's cradle there, where the lady lays the dogs, on
a soft cover, until they are ready to be cremated. There is a
visitors' book and we had the dogs' names entered and the
date they died. It was so lovely there and after tears we felt
we'd left our dogs in a place of rest and peace.

Hannah

Everyone I spoke to found the ritual of burial or cremation
tremendously healing. Perhaps it put a full stop to the end of their
pet's life. Or perhaps it simply meant that there was some kind of
memorial which lived on.

As the writer in the *Strand Magazine* wrote, when talking about
Centi, a little dog of 12 years who was buried in Hyde Park Pet
Cemetery: 'For 12 years Centi had been a faithful and affectionate
companion. How many human beings would have shown the like
constancy? And now he is gone, and all that is left of him is a tiny
mound of earth and a diminutive marble tombstone. Twelve years
is a slice out of one's life. It is nearly half a generation. The
friendships formed and the associations made for such a period are
not easily effaced, and can never be replaced. That, indeed, is the
saddest feature of the whole question of pets. They are short-lived.
One has scarcely time to grow fond of them, to find them entwined
in our hearts, before they are rudely wrenched away from us by the
cruel hand of Death.'

Chapter 6

⊗⊗⊗

'It Was Only an Animal!'

'I was sitting in the garden one day, thinking about how much I missed Sherry, listening to a country and western programme on the radio. The disc jockey announced he had a request for Old Shep. And then he said: "Who wants to talk about dead dogs on a lovely sunny Sunday afternoon?" It really hurt me. If only he knew what he had said.'

Susie

'It wasn't long after I was widowed that I had people coming up to me and saying: "Are you feeling better now?" "Now you must go out now and get married again!"' says Katie Boyle. 'If they're going to be insensitive about a partner, mother or father dying, what are they going to be like with a dog? They're going to say: "Oh, for God's sake, it's only a dog!"'

The loss of a pet is made all the worse by tactless remarks from other people. And the fact that other people seem to think that the number of tears you shed for a much-loved pet is somehow related to the size of the animal rather than the amount of love you had for each other, makes it worse. So often, in their confused minds, they seem to argue irrationally that the death of a mouse, rat or goldfish should take you only a couple of days to get over; a cat or a dog – a week; a horse, perhaps a fortnight; and a person a couple of months.

Then there's the problem of what to say. Most British people are uptight enough when it comes to saying anything when a husband or wife dies. We've all heard about those who cross to the other side of the road when seeing a bereaved person, too tongue-tied to offer any comforting words. So how on earth can they be expected to be sympathetic when your pet has died? It's made all the more difficult, in the case of a pet death, because probably they didn't know your pet as anything except a bundle of fur or feathers, whereas they might have known at least something of the personality of your parent or partner. And because we don't talk much about our pets socially to other people, and since pets themselves are not verbal and we communicate with them only by feelings, touch, feeding and play, the difficulty for others to empathise with our loss is compounded. They can't say: 'I'll always remember the time when . . .' about your pet, because they *don't* remember *any* times. The only people who *really* knew your pet were you and your family.

And even they can be very unsympathetic:

> I planned, for weeks and weeks, my dog's death, my
> terrible deed. I have no idea how I went through with it, I
> can't even kill a fly. No one in the family knew and the vet
> arrived late and it was all over so quickly. The vet told me
> to talk to him, but I couldn't use my normal voice so I'm
> sure he knew. Anyway it was all too quick by half, one
> minute he was awake, then his paw slipped and he was
> asleep (well, dead). The vet said I was 'brave'. But my

daughter called me a murderer and it took a long time for
her to speak to me again.

Kylie

My cat Tigger died last year and I can't look at his photo
or think of him without crying. I can't tell my family why
because the few times I have they look at me as if I am
mad.

Pauline

Then there are the people who get angry with an owner for
grieving over a pet. They take it personally and translate the grief
they feel over a lost cat or dog into indifference over human beings.

My uncle said: 'Well, it's only a dog, I've lost my wife,'
and when our next dog died and my uncle was ill with
cancer, he said: 'She was lucky, I've got to suffer!' It caused
me to feel guilty, but why should I? Our dogs were much
loved members of our family, yet I loved my uncle and
aunt and grieve for them, too.

Pat

In his book, *Resident Alien*, Ian Whitcomb describes a friend's
reaction after the death of his dog, Beefy. 'He was sympathetic
about Beefy and I suppose he was trying to help when he said that
we're all – humans and animals – just types, and there's plenty more
where we came from and probably a few models of me living
around the world – and certainly several in Britain. I thanked him
but I didn't believe a word. I felt certain of my own inexorable self.'

When I printed a letter on my problem page about a woman
who was mourning her cat and wanted its ashes to be buried with
her, I got a furious letter in response.

The person who wishes her cat's ashes to be buried with
her states 'It's like losing a child.' I can only assume she has
no children or she would not make such a stupid remark.
As a mother who lost her only son of 12 in 1949 from
kidney trouble, I can assure her there is no comparison.
The heartbreak and loss have never gone away. I too have
lost loved pets. You can replace them. But a loved child,
never. When I hear people say: 'It's like losing a child' over
a cat or dog, it makes me feel like screaming: 'You just
haven't a clue.'

Perhaps the saddest story, which pointed up how insensitive
others can be, came from Terry:

My dog's name was Ben, and I had him from a six-week-
old pup, and trained him, with my walking friends and
their dogs. He was very obedient and he would shake a
paw and he loved the grandchildren. If I had not had Ben I
don't think I would be here today. We used to go walking
from 8.15 to about 11 across fields, round by the
monastery in the forest, and the temptation now is to sleep
late, but I still go out with my mates and their dogs,
though I will not have another dog. I am now seventy and
that dog was so great to be with. I even built a conservatory
for him, complete with gas heater in the winter – he was
one of the family. I was out with my mates and one chap
asked where my dog was and when I told him he said, 'It
was only a dog – you can get another,' and I am afraid
things got unpleasant. But I will not speak to him again. I
am having to write this while my wife is in the bath. I have
got tears in my eyes writing this. And I don't want her to
comfort me – I have to be alone when I feel so unhappy.

And there's such an element of uncertainty – even about one's own reactions. In my time I've had about six cats put down without blinking an eye, but when my neighbour's cat died from falling off a piece of scaffolding I was extremely upset. You can be fairly sure with people that if someone close dies they will be unhappy. But you can't predict what anyone will feel about the death of a pet. Or they may feel nothing about the death of several pets and then suddenly the death of another will hit them like a blow from an axe. The fact that pets are legally regarded as property doesn't help, either. It makes so many non-pet owners see losing a pet in much the same terms as losing a pen or an umbrella.

But even professionals can put their foot in it. People have written to me at the problem page saying that they contacted CRUSE – which is the charity that helps bereaved people – for help over the death of an animal, and have been totally dismissed. 'We don't counsel people over pet deaths,' they've been told. That's why Suzanne Thomas says she feels that pet death is 'one of the most neglected areas of human grief there is. I discovered a few years ago that a lot of people are getting pretty raw deals when they're trying to talk about the loss of an animal. And, oddly enough and shockingly enough, from bereavement counsellors. One must remember that a dog can be like a child to someone and yet no one would consider dismissing the death of a child.'

So how *can* another person help? 'What people who have lost a pet want is to be taken seriously – and also to talk about what their pet was like,' she says. 'They can go on for ages about how their dog chased sticks thrown into ponds and how sometimes he would get it and sometimes he wouldn't, you could never tell, and a lot of people listening to that would think it was trite and ridiculous – but so what? It's most important to listen to stuff like that, however boring it is. People are allowed to tell other people about what their husband's favourite food was or what holiday he liked best – no one would think that was trite or ridiculous – but if someone tries to describe the warm feeling of a dog's paw on their foot they're dismissed as dull.'

Just knowing there's someone to talk to can help – even if people never take advantage of the help available. 'I often meet people who've been given my card by their vet and they say: "I didn't use it but it felt good to have it,"' says Suzanne. 'Knowing there was someone around who would take their feelings seriously was help enough in itself.

'In one practice where I worked, a little note would be sent to the owner of every pet that died, saying they were really sorry and if the owner wanted to come in and discuss it then please do – and they got a marvellous response.'

Members of your family who may react in a way you didn't expect are none other than your remaining pets, if you have any. If an animal is taken to the vet to be put down, it is frequently extremely confusing for the surviving animal, who may imagine his friend is lost. This is why some vets recommend that the remaining pet be shown the body of the dead animal so that it knows what has happened.

Averil Jarvis, of the Cinnamon Trust says: 'If a pet loses an animal friend it tends to grieve much more than if it loses an owner. The pets had particular games and even in love-hate relationships when you have a couple of cats spending their lives love-hating each other, when one dies the other is lost, it has no one to love-hate and it misses it.'

Sometimes the surviving animal is the comfort that no one else can be. Other people may make insensitive remarks about 'it was only a cat or a dog' but animals never say such things. They comfort in a non-verbal way, even though they may be suffering themselves.

No one understood how I felt, but my other cat, Smokey, was also bereft of his companion of ten years and he walked from room to room looking for Tinker and howling pitifully for many weeks. He and I spent many an hour cuddling and crying together in the ensuing months.

Margie

Chapter 7

Memorials – and Comfort

'We would say that there are various places in which a dog may be buried . . . beneath a cherry tree . . . on a hill . . . beside a stream . . . in the flatness of a pasture lane. But there is one place to bury a dog.

'If you bury him in this spot, he will come to you when you call – come to you over the grim, dim frontiers of death and down the well-remembered path and to your side again. And though you call a dozen living dogs to heel they shall not growl at him, nor resent his coming, for he belongs there. People may scoff at you who see no lightest blade of grass bent by his footfall, who hear no whimper, people who never really had a dog. Smile at them, for you shall know something that is hidden from them, and which is well worth the knowing. The one best place to bury a good dog is in the heart of its master.'

> Reply to a question in the *Ontario Argus* and
> quoted in *Pet Loss* by Herbert A. Nieburg and
> Arlene Fischer (Harper and Row, 1982)

Pets' deaths are rarely marked by any ceremony. Pet funerals are few and far between – and who writes condolence letters on the death of a pet? There are no memorial services, no wills, no rituals at all. This lack of 'full stop' to a pet's life can often result in owners becoming 'stuck' in their grief. But there are so many ways to commemorate a pet – as these ideas show.

Headstones

Plaques and headstones are fitting memorials for a much-loved pet. Indeed, recent advances in technology have allowed the pet's photograph to be engraved on a memorial plaque or stone. Some people like to have their animal's favourite toy – a teddy bear or ball – engraved into the stone as well.

One stonemason who specialises in pets' memorials, says: 'I mainly do dogs and cats, but occasionally one for a rabbit or a mouse. What is lovely about doing this job is that you are immortalising your client's pet. It's everlasting – like the pyramids. I did a stone for my wife's dog and when she looks out of the window and sees it in the garden she feels it's still with her.'

He takes great pride in his work, rather despising those who churn them out 'like kippers in a box. I'm not like that,' he said. 'Each stone is individually carved by hand. Each one means something special. People take a long time deciding about having a memorial. The other day I got an order from some people whose pet had died ten years ago.'

Another stonemason makes headstones, crosses and plaques and caters particularly for people 'who haven't got a garden or who are disabled or elderly. We do things like wooden clocks, personalised by the choice of flowers engraved on it; we have a ceramic urn for the ashes, and we also do caskets and coffins. We have made headstones for rabbits, budgies and cockatoos as well as dogs and cats.

'A lot of people are very upset, but they say that making their own inscription helps, because of instead of pushing it to the back of their minds, it makes them think what the animal meant.

'It all started when my husband's dog, Shadow, died. I made him a headstone – a concrete disc covered with hand-painted flowers with an inscription on it – and we haven't looked back.'

Here are some inscriptions from the gravestones at the Cambridge Pet Crematorium:

> In memory of Honeysuckle, our dear rabbit
> Stinks, I love and miss you baby doll, God bless you baby,
>   Mummy X
> Paws, our gentle giant, forever loved, always missed, the
>   family Rasch
> Bye Bruce, mum's babe, Sheila Sharon
> In loving memory of Radish, the little terror

A message for the blind

A gravestone for a guide dog has 'A real angel' written in Braille on the stone.

Garden memorials

Many people bury their pets in their gardens – and then plant a shrub or a tree over the grave. Some insert plaques into the walls, or even put up a special garden ornament to commemorate their pet's life, like Angela.

'We buried her in a box in the garden and bought a bird-bath which we put on her little place. The words on the bottom are: "Find much joy in earthly place. And in this spirit keep forever peace." I see it from my kitchen window.'

Keeping the ashes

It is often comforting to have a pet individually cremated and keep the ashes, as another Angela testifies: 'I now have Mandy's ashes back in a little carved casket with a brass plate on it. Her name and date are engraved on it. I have it by my bed so when I go to meet my maker she will go with me. I still miss her badly, like the day I arrived home from holiday she was not there to greet me. I missed her awfully then, no tail wagging, no bark and no big licks for me – it really hit me hard.'

Some people ask for their pets' ashes to be buried with them when *they* die. Since pets are seen as possessions like rings or letters, there is no reason why a clergyman should refuse permission for your pet's ashes to be buried with you. But make it clear to your nearest and dearest that this is what you want and don't just put the request in your will. By the time the will is read you'll hopefully already be six foot under.

Shrines

Keeping a shrine for your pet at home is not usual, but here is an example of someone who has done just that.

> The vet wrote a lovely letter saying that Dougal lived like a king and we had him cremated and his ashes are in a casket which we have put in our wall unit and turned into a shrine for him. We both feel that when we go, Dougal's ashes will go with whoever goes last. The reason we have not laid him to rest yet is in case we moved so he would always be with us. He showed more love and respect in his behaviour towards us than most humans we have known.
>
> *Denise*

A proper funeral

Although I said at the beginning of this chapter that most people had to find other ways of marking their pet's death since pet funerals aren't common, some owners refuse to lay their pet to rest without a proper ceremony.

One man in Georgia, USA, had a pet terrier whose funeral included the reading of scripture over an embalmed body, five dozen rosebuds, four pallbearers and a funeral procession of several cars for a total cost of $1,000. The owner, denying that his actions were extravagant, apparently asked reporters: 'Who else in the world has found a million dollars' worth of happiness for a thousand dollars?'

And, nearer home, the Shukla family in Blackburn, Lancashire, felt a funeral was appropriate when their dog, Bobo, died. 'When her liver started to fail, we took her to the vet but finally she stopped eating or drinking anything and in the end the vet said that though she wasn't in pain it might be sensible to consider putting her down – she was thirteen,' says Magda, the daughter of the family. 'It was a very difficult time for us because in our Hindu religion we believe we have no right to take the life of anything we have not given birth to because God is the giver of all life. Luckily we didn't have to make the decision, she just died a peaceful death at home. Because we treated her as part of the family we felt she should go respectfully with dignity. I was told we could hold a private cremation – but we wanted a proper funeral, so I phoned round undertakers. We said we were prepared to pay whatever it would cost and the funeral parlour was absolutely fantastic about it. We wanted a hearse and everything. We carried out the ceremony as for a human being, with a purification ceremony that we did at home; then we went to the cemetery where she was cremated and gathered her ashes and threw them into the Blackpool sea.

'Oh yes, we had a proper funeral procession, with the funeral car and the rest of the family members following. It was like we lost a family member.

'The people at the cemetery actually rang me up and wanted to film it all. And they did. We just feel okay she has died and gone and because there was publicity about it we feel that other people who feel the same way about their pets know that other people can do it. If you are prepared to do it it can be done.'

Action

Dr Mary Stewart quoted a case where just *doing* something healed one girl's grief. 'When she had heard of her dog's death she had lost consciousness after being hysterical. When she recovered, her boyfriend made her dig the grave herself and put the dog's body in it. She said the work helped her to face reality. On the gravestone she wrote: "Here lies Love."'

Religion

I go into this subject in much greater detail later, but there is no question that religion can be a great comfort to those who believe. For those who 'don't know', listen to this story from Averil Jarvis: 'A friend of mine had a friend who was dying. He had had a long-time argument with the local vicar about whether dogs went to heaven. His dog pre-deceased him by several years. This man finally went into a coma for several days. Suddenly he opened his eyes and grinned, smiling from ear to ear and said: "You can tell the bloody vicar there *are* dogs in heaven!" and he died. And he died with a smile on his face.'

Obituaries

Beverley Cuddy, the editor of *Dogs Today*, has had an obituary column from the first issue. 'We were very concerned to start with that it might be too morbid, but when you take on a pet you know it's got a shorter lifespan than you. It's bound to die first. We run a regular column on pet loss and when we did a survey we found that the content on bereavement is the most popular part of the magazine. So many people feel so strongly when their pet dies, but they have no voice. In our column they *do* have a voice to celebrate the time with their pets and mark it in some way.

'The service is quite free. It seemed so awful to charge people when they're pouring their heart out.

'And the obituaries are so much fresher than the ones people put in for their relatives. Sometimes they might refer to weird kinds of medical problems, like, "You didn't have tripsin but you did have love" and you find tripsin is some kind of pancreatic juice. So many people just don't realise how attached they are to a pet until it goes.'

Here are some of the obituaries from *Dogs Today*:

> RUFF (North Staff/Bull Terrier) – had to be put to sleep after being badly savaged by unmuzzled Pit Bull terrier. I love my sunbeam to pieces, no words could ever express how much I miss him, he was my life. A cuddle and a thousand kisses, you ever loving Irene, Ethel, Selina.

> Treasured memories of my beloved BONNY, a black cocker Spaniel bitch aged 23½ years; tragically killed while on her lead and on the pavement. I love you, miss you and grieve for you each day. Until we meet again, love Claire.

> KIP, forgive me. I knew what I had to do was best for you. It would have been wrong to let you go naturally but I feel a traitor. If they don't let dogs into heaven then I don't want to go. Your mind is now free from your worn-out body. I'll come to find you and the others one day. Wait for me. Mum and Co.

SHAYNE – I can't believe it's two years since you left me,
but in my heart you live on forever. We had 18 wonderful
years together. You helped me grow up and taught me so
much with your love. We will be together soon, wee man.
Wait for me, son, love Mum xxxxx (Michelle).

Pro-Rat-A, the National Fancy Rat Society Journal, has a column
of Hatches, Matches and Dispatches. Here are two charming
obituaries to rats:

LOOT (July 1989 – 16 January 1992) A shy gentleman
who loved his food. Put to sleep because of cancer. Now
reunited with brother Nailer. Thank you for keeping me
company. I shall not forget you.

SPLASH (June 1989 – 2 June 1991) A hooded buck, the
best little friend we've ever had. We are grateful to have
known a great character like him. 'You brought a splash of
happiness to our lives.' Now that he is reunited with his
parents, Putzi and Slash, he will still always remain right
here with us in our hearts. Love for ever, XXX

Pictures

Photographs can be enlarged and framed – apparently people
particularly like the frames lined with satin or velvet, a sensual
material like the muzzles of the dogs that are often portrayed. But
some owners get comfort from seeing their pets represented, from
photos, in oils.

'The problem is that people frequently come to me when they
only have one or two photos of animals which are rather blurred
and in the distance,' says Isobel Clark, of Coventry, a pet portrait

artist. 'But you get marvellous feedback. I sent one gentleman a portrait of his dog by recorded delivery. He went to collect it at the post office, opened it, and burst into tears in front of all his friends!

'It can be very difficult, of course, if you've never known the dog. I had one man who only had a tiny photo and he came to the house and described it to me and I showed it to him at all stages and slowly we got it right.'

Another pet portrait artist, says: 'You can bring out special features in a painting that just aren't there in a photograph. People love the paintings as a permanent reminder of their pet. Obviously if they're not happy with it I won't charge them – but no one's ever been dissatisfied yet. They often burst into tears when they see it.'

Freezing

The Cryonics Institute in the USA will suspend your pet in liquid nitrogen so that if we ever find out how to revive creatures after death, they can be brought back to life. The process is extremely expensive starting at $6,000.

Taxidermy

The idea of getting your pet stuffed may give some people the creeps – but though it's pretty expensive, it's not uncommon. A familiar sight in the 1930s was Lady Munnings who had a rather unpleasant peke. When it died, she had it stuffed and carried the animal around with her, even to the Lord Mayor's dinner. 'I remember seeing her in the King's Road carrying this creature,' says Katie Boyle. 'It was rather nauseating – bald in the places where she had been handling it too much.'

Robert Sinclair of Get Stuffed in London, says: 'We get quite a few people wanting their pets stuffed. We tell them if they can put their animal in the freezer for a few months they can then make a sensible decision about how to deal with it. They're always very pleased with the result. They don't want their animals to go into the earth and rot away. They particularly like their animal stuffed in a sleeping position, so you wouldn't know the difference, so they can stroke it.'

Jewellery and ornaments

Wearing something close to you that bears a reminder of your pet can often bring comfort.

> I've had a plain gold heart-shaped locket made with 'Buffy' inscribed on the front, and inside I have some of her ashes. I wear it day and night so that I can feel she is near me.
>
> Dawn

And one lady loved her pet marmoset so much that when she died, her owner had her cremated and her ashes sealed in a heart-shaped paperweight.

A jersey?

This is a very off-the-wall idea – but rather a splendid one . . .

> I always brushed my chow-chow and Labrador cross regularly and during the twelve years we had her I managed to collect enough fur combings to spin them on my spinning wheel. Eventually I knitted it all into a sleeveless pullover which I wear in the cold weather.
>
> Donna

Toys

If you've lost your pet and for some reason can't have another one — perhaps you've moved to a small flat or you can't afford another pet — you might follow the example of this lady who lost her cat: 'I have tiger pictures all round the walls in my bedroom and I know it sounds daft but I would just like to go up to a tiger and give him one big cuddle, just to give that animal my human feeling of love for it. To me, as wild as they are, they seem such lovely animals. I say to my husband: "I know it's impossible to want to cuddle a tiger but if only there were some way, I would — because they come from the cat family." I have a toy stuffed tiger that sits on my bed that my husband bought me for Christmas. He said it's the nearest he could give me to that feeling. You might not believe it but it does wonders for me.'

Poems

I have received hundreds of poems over the years that people have written to commemorate the death of their pets. Perhaps they don't always scan, perhaps the rhymes are a bit dodgy, but they're all unfailingly heart-rending. As Bianca said after the death of her pets: 'I wrote these poems and somehow it helped to ease the heartache I felt. And for those who have lost a beloved pet I suggest they write a letter to their pet and describe their feelings in it, or make a "pretend" telephone call to them expressing their love and grief. Too often human friends are unable to understand the depths of grief a pet lover suffers.'

This is a long poem by Nadia Carre written on the death of one of her pet rats. She has actually written several other poems to celebrate the lives and deaths of all of them, and I'm only sorry I can't reproduce them all. But this, I think, shows exactly how much Nadia felt for her friend.

For Mitzie Rat

My rodent friend what of your life?
The babies' mum and Boysie's wife.
I'll begin at the start
One look from you, you stole my heart.
Your soft brown eyes they said to me
'Please take us home and set us free
From this life of misery!'

Your fur was dull, you body thin,
Someone was cruel, that was a sin.
At first you liked to bite my hand,
I found it hard to understand.
I gave you treats I kept you clean,
I'd watch you sleep and feed and preen.
Then one fine morn, what did I see?
Six jelly babies squeaky clean
Your motherhood was unexpected
You never left them unprotected.
At first I was not amused
But when it came the time to choose
Which to go and which to stay
I kept them all anyway.

From then you changed from wild to tame,
You never bit my hand again.
Your coat it shone, your tummy round,
A kindly home you had found,
With all your family around.

The last few months you knew no fear,
You trusted me, I'd kiss your ear.

Then one sad day you passed away.
I cradled you within my arms
And reminisced upon your charms
My chest I thought would rent in two
I gasped for breath at losing you.
I placed you in the hallowed ground
And said goodbye without a sound.
A peaceful resting place you've found.

I once had eight but now it's seven,
I know your soul's in ratty heaven.
I miss you still, I always will
Each tear a tribute to your life
The babies' mum and Boysie's wife,
You left me with a gift of joy
Three pretty girls, three handsome boys,
Each one of them a pure delight
They love to play and fuss and fight.

You may have been just a rat
But to me much more than that.
If you are watching it's to see
I'm caring for them properly.
Whilst your life was sometimes tragic
Theirs for sure is truly magic.
Your mate lives on in luxury
Your young are free from misery.
I know that you'll be pleased with that
My much-mourned Mitzie Rat.
You were indeed a special friend
And friendship lasts until the end.

Memories

Remembering the happy times with pets can sometimes help owners from getting too upset.

> Every time I go into the kitchen where Bob slept I feel the
> emptiness because Bob's not there, but I smile as I
> remember all the great times we had together. Bob didn't
> last for ever, like so many things, but the memories of him
> will and that's what helps me through my bereavement.
>
> *Melinda*

Denial

Denial's often seen as a bad thing, but if it brings comfort why not? Why not talk to a cat or dog that's not there? It's harmless – and if it's comforting, go for it!

> We sometimes slip up, drop a titbit on the floor for our
> three dogs, forgetting they aren't there. Yesterday we went
> on a pensioners' trip to Hatfield House in Herts and one
> of the marquees was full of dogs' equipment and I said to
> my hubby: 'Shall we buy a thermal blanket for Brownie's
> rheumaticky legs?' He said: 'We haven't got the dogs now,
> dear.'
>
> *Meriel*

> Lots of people think I'm crazy to grieve over her but
> nursing and loving her as I did for nineteen years I feel I'm
> entitled to. I still say: 'Night, night, Suki, God bless' every
> night and still talk to my other cat, Herby and my dog, Jo
> Jo, about her and I'm sure they understand the heartache
> I'm suffering.
>
> *Catherine*

Rebel died last year after eighteen years of fun. It was real humour which transformed her whole little body into vibrant animation when she felt we too were seeing the funny side of something. She became a tail-wagging mass of jollity. But then it ceased. After her final visit to the vet I returned to my car and started a conversation which has never really ended. 'Going home now, darling, and then we'll go walkies later!' 'Oh, look! There's another doggie!' and so on. The photograph has flowers beside it because I taught her to 'sniff' the perfume of flowers when I was in the garden, and two noses would waggle in appreciation. Approaching home, I say, as I always did, 'Straight down the road, one more corner, another straight bit and yippee! We're home!' Somehow her excitement still permeates my day.

Verconica

Thoughts for double grief

Averil Jarvis has these wise thoughts for people suffering from what's called 'double grief – that is when a woman – or man – loses a partner and then, some years later, their dog.

'When the pet is still there it's a sort of bridge to the lost partner,' she says. 'I try and comfort people by saying that when it dies, the pet is with the husband now, they can talk to them both, they're both there in spirit. And most important, now he has got his pet in heaven, you can now have yours on earth – so get another one! Remember that they had special games and think of them doing them now, wherever they are together. People often have little rituals with their pets, like at cocoa time he had a chocolate biscuit and the dog had half and I always suggest they think of them doing it together every time cocoa time comes around. Eventually that memory comes with a smile and you learn to live with it.'

Pet bereavement counselling

Some ordinary bereavement counsellors will talk to you if you're very depressed about the death of an animal. And it really is worth getting in touch with expert help if the grief over an animal's death is getting unmanageable. See the back of the book for agencies that provide exclusive pet bereavement counselling.

Coming to terms – sadly

This is a tragic tale of a woman from Blackpool who has tried so many things to ease her pain and ended up by having, simply, to live with her grief. She suffered from infertility and then her kitten, Feather, died in a car accident. She has tried many of the suggestions offered in this chapter – but her conclusion is just to bear her pain as bravely as possible.

> My initial reaction was one of horror and disbelief. I kept walking round in circles trying to escape the terrible pain I felt. My husband buried her under the apple tree in the garden. I felt my life had ended there and then and that I no longer wanted to live. I would leave food outside the door in case she was hungry and I would lie out in the garden just to be near her. As the weeks went on I became more and more like a zombie – I didn't want to get up or see anyone or go anywhere. I just wanted to die. Apart from my family and closest friends, people were insensitive, saying I should get another one. My own mother-in-law said, the day after Feather died: 'Oh, well, it's over now, forget about it.' Yet my good friend whose own son had killed himself at the age of seventeen never once diminished my grief – she listened to hours of my torment with patience and understanding and she equated my experience with her own. I bought a shrub which was

in flower at the time of Feather's death – an azalea called
Mother's Day – and I planted it on her grave so that it
would flower every year. I started to write down all my
thoughts and express my innermost feelings in poetry. I
gradually built up a series of poems and made them into a
book which I covered with white satin and lace. I
included lots of things that were Feather's – like her
collar, a whisker that I'd found around the house, and
photographs. It made me feel closer to her. But after
nearly a year I felt I couldn't go on so my husband took
me to the doctor. I was so bad I could hardly speak – I
just cried. My husband explained and I was diagnosed as
being clinically depressed. I saw a psychiatrist and had
several sessions of group therapy etc. but none of it did
any good. Other people in the group thought I was raving
mad to be in this state over a cat. I stopped going. In the
meantime I treated my husband and family as if they
didn't exist. I stopped going to the group and for two
years every night I hoped I wouldn't wake up the next
morning. I went for long solitary walks so that I would
feel close to nature and therefore closer to Feather. Then
one night I decided to go to our spiritualist church and it
did help. I began to look on Feather's death in a different
light and found comfort in the belief that she was at peace
in paradise. After two years I decided I might as well try
to get on with living. I booked a driving lesson the next
day and learnt to drive and from that day my life became
more normal. We now have two other cats but I am
different now and know I will never be as happy as I was
before this happened. This experience changed my
personality. It is like a nightmare that never goes away, it
just lurks in the background of my life.

I have a photograph of Feather in a crystal frame next to where I sit in the living room and, behind it, there's a tiny crystal vase where I have put a fresh flower every day for nine years. I still say goodnight to her every night before I go to bed. We never did have children but I feel as if I came as close to it as I could by having my little Feather.

Coming to terms – happily

This is a long letter from Pam in the form of a diary, but I'm sure it will bring comfort to the many people who mourn. It shows clearly grief as a series of stages.

I had a wonderful husband, daughter, son and two adored grandchildren. But for nine years I got the most tremendous joy out of my lovely golden cocker spaniel. She died suddenly on the settee beside me. For three months the pain was unbearable. I had felt grief at the loss of my mother and father who I had dearly loved, but this was different, it was actually worse and I felt so guilty about that. Several times a day I cried. I would go for a walk to a place where I used to take her which was away from houses, it was very open, and I could see there was no one around and I would cry out loud, almost howl. Entering the house was one of the worst things – going through the front door to silence, after nine years of a rapturous welcome. I had to get through the lounge and into the kitchen where I would sob until I ached. Then pull myself together before anybody else came in. All the family adored Suki so they all suffered but I just could not come to terms with it.

Nobody wanted to talk to me about Suki for fear of upsetting me more. But all I wanted to do was talk about her. So I began writing about her and it was wonderful therapy. For the first few days after her death I was like a zombie. I would disappear into my bedroom and sob till I fell asleep exhausted. Everywhere I looked in the house I visualised her there. I imagined her running to meet me up the lane with her big floppy ears flying. I would be crouched with my arms open while waiting to hug her. Then she would twirl round all the way back to the house yelping in delight. Gone forever.

I kept as busy as I could to get my mind off her, to give it a rest. But really she was there all the time, just tucked away in the corner. Three months passed and I was still torn inside. Most nights in bed I could never suppress the tears squeezing through and onto the pillow. I thought I was getting over it but it isn't a steady progress. One seems to progress and then regress.

Six months on nobody knew the depth of my misery. I was trying my very best to snap out of it. I missed the very essence of her, something that was more than the sight, sound and touch of her. Just when I was feeling all right I found a little bunch of her dog hairs tucked into the edge of the stair carpet. I held them between my fingers, soft and silky, and a hundred memories flashed across my mind.

Seven months and I was feeling quite good. I could look at her photograph without a lump in my throat. But two weeks later I wasn't feeling so good. So many things were there to remind me of the wonderful days we shared. I would take her to the post office just two hundred yards from my house and hitch her lead to a post outside. I couldn't bear to look at that post. What a bitter pill it is to swallow, when you know that however you long, however much you yearn, nothing but nothing can alter the facts.

Five years after she died, the field at the back is full of barley – she is buried in a corner. It has been raining continually for two days, everywhere is sodden. It's impossible to reach Suki's plot. Oh, to think five years have passed! The pain has long gone but the memory of her hasn't dimmed. My three-year-old grandson had come across Suki's lead and attached it to his little jeans saying he was a doggie. I held the lead and followed him around and smiled to myself.

Inscription on the Monument of a Newfoundland Dog

When some proud son of man returns to earth
Unknown to glory, but upheld by birth,
The sculptor's art exhausts the pomp of woe,
And storied urns record who rest below;
When all is done, upon the tomb is seen
Not what he was, but what he should have been;
But the poor dog, in life the firmest friend,
The first to welcome, foremost to defend,
Whose honest heart is still his master's own,.
Unhonour'd falls, unnoticed all his worth
Denied in heaven, the soul he held on earth;
While man, vain insect! hopes to be forgiven,
And claims himself a sole exclusive heaven.
Oh man! thou feeble tenant of an hour,
Debased by slavery, or corrupt by power,
Who knows thee well must quit thee with disgust.
Degraded mass of animated dust!
Thy love is lust, thy friendship all a cheat,
Thy smiles hypocrisy, thy words deceit!
By nature vile, ennobled but by name,
Each kindred brute might bid thee blush for shame.
Ye! who perchance behold this simple urn,
Pass on – it honours none you wish to mourn;
To mark a friend's remains these stones arise;
I never knew but one – and here he lies.

Byron

Epitaph on a Favourite Dog

Thou who passes on the path; if haply thou dost mark this monument, laugh not I pray then, though it is a dog's grave; tears fell for me and the dust was heaped above me by a master's hands who likewise engraved these words on my tomb. (From a Greek Anthology trans. by J.W. Mackail.)

Chapter 8

⬡⬡⬡

Do They Go To Heaven?

'When the hold was ready, Durbeyfield and his wife tied a rope round the horse and dragged him up the path towards it, the children following in funeral train. Abraham and 'Liza-Lu sobbed, Hope and Modest discharged their griefs in loud blares which echoed from the walls; and when Prince was tumbled in they gathered round the grave. The bread-winner had been taken away from them; what would they do?

"'Is he gone to heaven?" asked Abraham, between the sobs.'

Tess of the d'Urbervilles by Thomas Hardy

The question of whether our animal friends pass through the pearly gates is one that vexes many bereaved pet owners. Do animals have souls? The founder of the Protestant church, Martin Luther, certainly believed they went to heaven. 'Be comforted, little dog,' he said. 'Thou too in the Resurrection, shall have a little golden tail.'

There are many references to animals in the Bible – including the words that 'God exists not only in man but in everything that lives'. And the lovely Benedicite is a song of worship in praise of all things that live:

> O ye Wells, bless ye the Lord: praise him, and magnify
> him for ever.
> O ye Seas and Floods, bless ye the Lord: praise him and
> magnify him for ever
> O ye Whales, and all that move in the Waters, bless ye
> the Lord: praise him and magnify him for ever.
> O all ye Fowls of the Air, bless ye the Lord: praise him
> and magnify him for ever.
> O all ye Beasts and Cattle, bless ye the Lord: praise him
> and magnify him for ever.
> O ye Children of Men, bless ye the Lord: praise him and
> magnify him for ever . . .

And so on, including priests of the Lord, servants of the Lord, green things upon the earth, winds, ice and snow etc.

Indeed, the very word 'animal' is derived from that of *anima* or soul. And yet although I, and I imagine most people reading this book, would not wish to go to a heaven that didn't have animals in it, I was surprised, when doing my research, to find the number of religious people who balked at the idea. Certainly historically animals have not found it at all easy to gain a passport to the afterlife.

Despite the fact that we can see plenty of tombs in cathedrals of knights who have dogs at their feet, no one really knows if they are in there as a sign of their spiritual qualities or as signs of fealty. And according to Blake Morrison writing in the *Independent on Sunday*: 'In medieval Europe, right through until the last century, there was widespread belief that . . . animals were the satellites of Satan. There are many instances of the Church excommunicating and anathematising animals. The Devil was an ass – or a cloven-hoofed goat, a raven, dog, fox, frog or weevil. Even the most innocuous of creatures came under suspicion. Egbert, Bishop of Trier, was so enraged by the chirpy disturbances of swallows that he forbade them to enter his cathedral on pain of death.'

One otherwise delightful clergyman told me: 'The basic distinction between animals and people is that it was people – Adam and Eve – who ate of the tree of knowledge of good and evil. We are the only ones who can look into the future and decide which moral course to take. And in that we have that knowledge, we are one step above the animals – and therefore they cannot enter heaven.'

Even vets aren't particularly open-minded. In one survey of vets, only 19 per cent believed that animals had souls.

Catholics have had a tricky time with the animal soul question – until January 1990 when Pope John Paul II came out with an astonishing statement. He said that 'also the animals possess a soul and men must love and feel solidarity with our smaller brethren'. This caused a tremendous kerfuffle in the Catholic Church. He pointed out that in Genesis ' . . . the way in which man was created suggests a relationship with the spirit or "breath" of God. And one reads that after having created man from the dust of the earth, the Lord God "breathed life into his nostrils and man became a living soul."' He went on to say that animals have the breath of life and were given it by God. So in this respect, man, created by the hand of God, is identical with all other living creatures.

Now the argument rages, apparently, about whether animals have 'immortal' souls or not, these, apparently, being different to 'ordinary' souls.

That champion of animal rights, John Austin Baker, the former Bishop of Salisbury is very anti-blood sports and generally believes that the Church has got a rotten record when it comes to caring about animal welfare. 'One of the appalling things about being an animal enthusiast like my wife and myself is that on the whole churches give animal welfare a very low priority.'

On the subject of whether animals have souls or not, he naturally takes a liberal view. 'Thomas Aquinas and the scholastic tradition said very clearly that animals have *not* got souls and this has been used in the past to justify any exploitation of animals on the grounds that they are just things,' he says. 'I don't think that any Christian church has officially said that animals enjoy personal immortality or will be resurrected for life in a future world in the way it is believed that people are – but that of course isn't the end of the story.

'Some people have said that what gives animals a place in heaven would be their relationship with human beings. If human beings get to heaven, then animals get carried along with them. But that puts paid to 99.9 per cent of all living creatures. The idea was that when people couldn't see or experience an animal's personality, it couldn't get into heaven. It was thought that animals' consciousness was so limited that they needed to be appendages of human beings to be capable of enjoying the life in heaven. But then what do we actually know about animal consciousness?

'You surely don't have to have high rational intelligence like human beings in order to have the possibility of a relationship to transcendent or eternal life.

'The idea that only humans can get to heaven because only they understand good and evil is very simplistic. Surely heaven is not a question of moral virtue. And even if it were, animals do have a sense of guilt, certainly pet dogs. They know there are certain things their owners disapprove of. You only have to say: "What have you been doing?" when they've been up to something wrong and they go down all grovelling and shamefaced.

'As for wild animals, there are a lot of human beings who are quite psychopathic or amoral or unable to make relationships – all of us are damaged to a certain extent – and these people can go off in appalling directions, but no one thinks that God cannot forgive and heal them and that they can't go to heaven.

'There isn't as much difference between human beings and animals as our old-fashioned picture used to give. Of course, we are much more highly organised and we have capacities that animals don't have – as they have capacities that we don't have – but nevertheless there are basic similarities. We are physical beings who have characters and ways of responding which are the result of our life history. It's therefore very difficult to draw a clear line and say, at least with regard to a large number of species of animals, that they are so different from human beings there could be no place for them in a closer relationship with God.'

So far, so good. But, curiously, the bishop feels that 'the line has to be drawn somewhere'. He quotes Hilaire Belloc's 'He prayeth best who loveth best all things both great and small, If streptococcus is the test I love him best of all,' and laughs, saying: 'I don't think we have to get down to that level because the function of many organisms is purely to service the general process of life. They have no consciousness. There are a great many quite complicated organisms which as far as we can see are not sentient and are purely mechanical. So I suppose if you're going to draw a line you probably would say that all the trillions of mosquitoes are unlikely to go to heaven, but no one is actually arguing about that.

'The question really is: what is heaven? If it's simply a kind of eternal holiday camp where you go as a reward for being good in this life, it would be very limited and there wouldn't be many people there anyway. I would say that there are no limits to the love of God and I can imagine no limits to its healing power and I imagine that all the twisted and damaged human beings can in fact be healed and able to grow by God's love, forgiveness and understanding in heaven. I can't see any limit to this so I can't see any limit to anything that has a potential for good. God will find a place for it; it's just that our imaginations are so limited and small we can't think how it could possibly be – but then we can't understand what we mean by God anyway.

'The key question is not "Do animals have souls or do animals qualify for heaven?" but what do you actually mean by "heaven"? If you imagine it as the fulfilment of perfection of the whole creation where all that is potentially good is brought to life in eternity in perfect harmony, then you can find heaven for anything you like – there isn't a problem.'

Several pet owners are anxious about whether their pets will be waiting for them in heaven.

> We are told that animals have no souls and cannot survive but I believe that a loving creator will not exclude those beautiful creatures that share our planet from the place we call heaven. I for one hope not anyway.
>
> Phil

And perhaps the final consolation, for anyone who isn't certain of meeting their beloved pet in the afterlife, comes from a bishop who comforted a bereaved parishioner with the words: 'You must always remember that as far as the Bible is concerned, God only threw the humans out of paradise.'

Getting into less orthodox areas – the worlds of spiritualism and psychic experiences – there's even more comfort to be found.

'Incredibly there are some who accept human survival after death but not that of animals, whom they foolishly and arrogantly call "dumb" or our "lesser brethren",' wrote Tony Ortzen, the former editor of *Psychic News*, in his introduction to *Animals in the Spirit World* by Harold Sharp. 'There is certainly nothing dumb about the majority of creatures; neither do I see any reason to regard them as spiritually less in stature than mankind. Indeed, it is mankind himself who often forgets he, too, is an animal that wreaks so much havoc, destruction and needless hurt upon this earth . . . I believe, as do countless others throughout the world, that life is spirit and spirit is life. Every creature that moves, lives and breathes on earth does so because it is activated by a spiritual force that nothing, not even so-called death, can extinguish. It is this vital spark of spirit that decrees survival after physical death for all sentient creatures no matter how low their intellect or humble their status in human terms. Life – and death – would be a total sham were God or a life force to decree that humans continue in a spiritual dimension whilst animals do not. The emotions and characteristics displayed by many animals often surpass those of supposedly civilised and advanced humans.'

Katie Boyle agrees: 'Perhaps I find one of my pet's deaths easier than some because I have no doubt at all that there is a continuity between this world and another. I have personal experiences to back this belief up,' she says. 'When I was a child of about thirteen or fourteen I actually watched someone come into the room and there were two dogs obviously with her, even though they weren't there. I couldn't believe it. I felt a whoosh of coldness which you always get when there's something from another world around, and my dogs' eyes followed these two creatures – and they left two small dents on the bed where they had been. They were definitely the dents of dogs. My dogs were fascinated. And then when they'd gone again my dogs looked up and their eyes followed them.'

Clive Jackman, of the Cambridge Pet Crematorium, told me: 'Once a spiritualist came for the cremation of her dog – though I didn't know she was a spiritualist at the time. And she kept looking at me. I thought there was something wrong me, checked my hair, my teeth, I got a bit of a complex after a while. Then she called me over and she said: "Do you know what, Mr Jackman? All around you are animals. When you pass over you will be greeted by thousands of dogs!" I said: "That can't be bad, I'll have some of that!"'

Here are some personal testimonies of psychic experiences with dead pets:

> Mikky, my Highland terrier, was everything to me. A year after his passing I was lucky enough to see the late Doris Stokes at Walthamstow Assembly Hall. Halfway through the show she said: 'I have a Mick here, does that mean anything to anybody?' and then she said: 'No, it's not Mick, it's Mikky and it's a dog.' With that I raised my hand and went to the stage. She told me what he passed over with and said I carried him about a lot which was true. So I do believe that love will always keep us both together, that bond will never break. I know his spirit is alive and one day we will be back together.
>
> Paul

> Trix had comforted me through so many crises – I cried many useless tears into his coat and he would push his nose into my lap, I told him all my woes and trials and shared good things, too. Eventually he had to be put to sleep. I do believe in an afterlife and sometimes I feel Trix is near. When I get distressed sometimes I hear him tap at the door as he always did and I have even got up thinking to let him in.
>
> Anne

Last week my Dalmatian bitch suddenly died an agonising death by poisoning. Because I have two other dogs I scoured the bathroom, where she died, with disinfectant. Since then, both Buster and Scruffy spend all their time in the bathroom, which they never did before. They seem quite contented, their attention on something I cannot see, with their tails wagging. They come out for meals and for walks and then go straight back into the bathroom, though as time passes they are not as desperate to get in there. There seems to be no explanation for they were not present when Keaton died and have shown no sign of missing her. They both dislike the smell of disinfectant and apart from this inexplicable behaviour they are exactly the same as ever.

William

My dog Leo had to have an operation and I arranged to have a tape of my voice sent in to him in an effort to make him fight as the vet couldn't understand why he wasn't recovering quicker. On the sixth night following the operation, I was lying in bed thinking about him and trying to talk to him telepathically (sounds silly but I didn't know what else to do) when I heard him come up the stairs and flop against my bedroom door, as he did every night. That's when I knew he'd died. And he had died at exactly that time when I checked with the vet. It's two and a half years now and I'm about to cover up the last trace of this wonderful dog – I'm going to paint over the large dirty mark on the wall where he would sit for hours, watching the world go by through a glass vestibule door! I never had the heart to wash it off. I sometimes think my cats see him, the way they suddenly stop what they're doing and gaze, as if mesmerised, by the dirty mark on the wall.

Elaine

Fifteen months after Suki's death one of my brothers-in-law, a very level-headed man, came on a visit. Three weeks later he called again and told me that on his previous visit, as he had entered the lounge, Suki was standing near the settee. Then she just turned and walked into the kitchen. He had completely forgotten our dog had died. It wasn't until his second visit that it hit him. Four years later we had a visitor who was showing us some of his paintings. He had been with us an hour when suddenly he said, surprised: 'Oh, you have a dog!' He had seen a dog quietly sitting inside the kitchen. When he realised we hadn't he kept saying: 'Oh, that's really knocked me back.' He was shocked, but we were delighted. Seven years after her death I had a surprise visit from my ex-daughter-in-law. As she was leaving and was about to go out of the front porch door she quickly stepped to the side as she felt a dog coming behind her. She saw the back of the dog as it passed her. She knew she had seen my Suki. She was visibly shaken. For me, who ached for the want of the sight of her, not a glimpse. But I can accept that now I can wait.

Sandra

I am seventy but well recall when I was seven we had a big black dog called Peter. He had been in the family since before I was born and we were very attached to each other. How I remember those days when Peter and I would romp and play together in the woods and fields that surrounded our country home! After he died I felt that life had lost its meaning; neither the woods nor the fields were lovely any more without him. I was raised as a Roman Catholic and it was no comfort to be taught then by the priests and

nuns that only human beings had immortal souls that lived
in another world after death. But then in my late teens I
was attracted to spiritualism. They taught that animals,
like humans, are immortal, that in the spirit they will be
the same as we will be when passed to the other side. One
medium described Peter and the times we had together
and said that he is some kind of spirit guide to me. After
several such clairvoyant messages I became convinced that
this was a far more bounteous religion, not mere promises,
but the reality brought directly and undeniably to one. No
orthodox preacher or indoctrinate would convince me that
it was some imp of the devil impersonating my beloved
Peter just to lead me astray.

*C*harlotte

I had a lovely little dog who died of cancer and I was
heartbroken. My son always wanted me to get another dog
but I couldn't bring myself to. Then my son died – he was
only 47 and I was seventy and I so wished I could have
gone first. Then a year later a wonderful thing happened. I
saw a lovely little dog in the road and as I passed by she
was wagging her tail and I stopped to give her a little
stroke and pat and went off on my errand. When I came
back she was there on my doorstep. I went to the police
but it turned out she was a little stray so I took her in. I'm
not a particularly religious person but I'm convinced my
son was able to send this little dog to me at that special
time to help me in my grief, which she did and still does.
She needed me and I needed her, we both love each other
very much.

*P*etra

In his book, *Animals in the Spirit World*, Harold Sharp tells of his experience with a disbelieving vicar. 'I asked him if I could place at the grave as a memorial (of a friend), a marble bird-bath with a carved inscription: "All things great and small – The Lord God made them all."

'The vicar was most indignant and refusing said: "It would lead to all sorts of wrong ideas." "That is not my wish," I said. "I hoped it would lead to all sorts of *right* ideas, and I am sure it would be very acceptable to the one in whose memory it was created." But this very orthodox vicar thought that as animals have no souls, the "faithful" in Heaven would cease to be interested in them; and in any case it might induce ignorant people on earth to think that animals in God's sight were as important as humans.

'A few years afterwards he "died" and I have often thought how surprised he must have been to discover in the heavenly courts that the text he must have frequently read – "Not one sparrow falleth to the ground but your Heavenly Father careth" – was no mere platitude. How shocked he must have been to find there not only sparrows but dogs and donkeys and indeed all the animals poor Adam – if tradition is reliable – had the unenviable job of naming.'

Even the author John Galsworthy had his tale to tell about a dog returning to its mistress: 'My companion tells me that, since he left us, he has once come back. It was Old Year's Night, and she was sad, when he came to her in visible shape of his black body, pattering round the dining-room from the window-end, to his proper place beneath the table at her feet. She saw him quite clearly; she heard the padding tap-tap of his paws and very toe-nails; she felt his warmth pressing hard against the front of her skirt. She thought then that he would settle down upon her feet but something disturbed him, and he stood pausing, pressed against her, then moved out toward where I generally sit, but was not sitting that night. She saw him stand there, as if considering; then at some sound or laugh, she became self-conscious, and slowly, very slowly, he was no longer there. Had he some message, some counsel to give, something he would say, that last night of the last year of all those he had watched over us? Will he come back again?

'No stone stands over where he lives. It is on our hearts that his life is engraved.'

Even the famous Konrad Lorenz wrote, in 1957: 'In the weeks following Bully's death, I really began to understand what it is that makes naïve people believe in the ghosts of the dead. The constant sound throughout seventeen years of my dog trotting at my heels had left such a lasting impression on my brain that for weeks afterwards as if with my own ears, I heard him pattering after me.'

Was this just a memory imprinted on his brain? Or was it really the ghost of Bully?

One of the saddest results of the argument about whether animals have souls or go to heaven is that they are nearly always denied proper religious funerals. There is no official ceremony to mark the end of an animal's life – although it is always worth devising one if it makes you feel better because some churches and vicars are less narrow-minded about the place of animals in the church than others.

'Even so, when it comes to burial, although there is no law that you can't bury an animal in consecrated ground, if you went to a vicar and asked to bury a dog or cat in a graveyard the answer would certainly be: "No",' says the former Bishop of Salisbury. 'But remember until recently you couldn't bury anyone who was not baptised or anyone who had committed suicide. Similarly, you would not get a funeral service.

'There's a boarding school in this diocese where the girls are encouraged to have pets and of course they do die from time to time and the headmistress takes a very severe attitude. She says they always want a little service and she says she always tries to "stop that kind of nonsense". But I was talking to her chaplain and I said: "I hope you're not taking this line" and he said: "Oh no, she doesn't know but we always have something. The girls want to express their grief and their gratitude and their hopes and it seems very inhuman not have something.'"

Wendy Perriam, in *The Things We Do for Love*, described the funeral she gave her dog, William. 'My second husband, a woodwork fiend, set about crafting his coffin – finest-grain mahogany, with brass handles and lined with a magnificent velvet curtain. His shroud was my best Harrods dressing gown. We filled his coffin with grave-goods, in the manner of Tutankhamen, to prepare him for the Other Side – a juicy marrowbone, chicken breast in jelly, chocolate Doggy Drops. I composed a funeral ode ... On a dark day in November, the funeral guests assembled in our garden – my parents, our three children, the neighbours from both sides and assorted friends and relatives. My daughter laid the wreath and my stepson was in charge of the cassette and soon the strains of Verdi's *Dies Irae* were thundering over the privet hedge. When I rose to deliver the funeral address, solemnising William's official passing to the Great Lamppost in the Sky, there was not a dry eye in the house.'

If you would like to give your animal a funeral service, this is a suggested form.

Opening prayer

O Lord, whose nature is love and who has asked us to love one another, you have blessed us with the companionship of animals. In their lives we have seen glimpses of the divine tenderness that you feel to all creation. Today we are here to remember one animal in particular – (your pet's) NAME. We want to thank you for his/her life, for the delight and pleasure of his/her presence among us, and for all the love and loyalty he/she showed to us, his/her family.

Hymn suggestions

> 'The King of Love my Shepherd is'.
>
> 'There's a wideness in God's mercy'.
>
> 'All things bright and beautiful'.
>
> 'Dear Lord and Father of Mankind'.
>
> 'Immortal, Invisible, God only wise'.
>
> 'Jesus shall reign where'er the sun'.

First lesson

The Prophet Isaiah's description of the holy mountain:

The wolf also shall dwell with the lamb, and the leopard shall lie down with the kid; and the calf and the young lion and the fatling together; and a little child shall lead them.

And the cow and the bear shall feed; their young ones shall lie down together; and the lion shall eat straw like the ox.

And the sucking child shall play on the hole of the asp, and the weaned child shall put his hand on the cockatrice' den.

They shall not hurt nor destroy in all my holy mountain; the earth shall be full of the knowledge of the Lord, as the waters cover the sea.

Isaiah II: 6–9.

Music or hymn

Burial prayer, if needed

As it has pleased God to take to himself our dear friend – NAME – we therefore commit his/her body to the ground; earth to earth, ashes to ashes, dust to dust; in the hope that we may meet again in that holy place where there shall be neither hurt not destruction.

Second lesson

St John the Divine's vision of heaven:

And I beheld, and I heard the voice of many angels round about the throne and the beasts and the elders; and the number of them was ten thousand times ten thousand, and thousands of thousands.

Saying with a loud voice, Worthy is the Lamb that was slain to receive power, and riches, and wisdom, and strength and honour, and glory and blessing.

And every creature which is in the heaven, and on the earth, and under the earth, and such as are in the sea and all that are in them, heard I saying: Blessing, and honour, and glory and power, be unto him that sitteth upon the throne, and unto the Lamb for ever and ever . . .

And I saw a new heaven and a new earth; for the first heaven and the first earth were passed away; and there was no more sea.

And I John saw the holy city, new Jerusalem, coming down from God out of heaven, prepared as a bride adorned for her husband.

And I heard a great voice out of the throne saying, Behold the tabernacle of God is with men, and he will dwell with them, and they shall be his peoples, and God himself shall be with them and be their God.

And God shall wipe away all tears from their eyes; and there shall be no more death; neither sorrow, nor crying, neither shall there be any more pain.

Revelation of St John 5: 11–12 and 21: 1–4

Reading suggestions

Epitaph by Lord Byron for his dog, Boatswain (see page 67) or:

Poem to His Dead Dog

Oh friend of man! Blest being! You that shared
Your master's hunger and his meals as well!
You that in days of old in pilgrimage fared
With young Tobias and the angel Raphael.

Servant that loved me with a love intense,
As saints love God, my great exemplar be!
The mystery of your strange intelligence
Dwells in a guiltless, glad eternity.

Dear Lord! If You should grant me by Your grace
To see You face to face in heaven, O then
Grant that a poor dog look into the face
Of him who was his God here among men.

Francis Jammes (translator unknown)

Address

A prayer for the departed and those that mourn:

O Lord, who cares for each sparrow that falls to the ground, grant – NAME – peace in your loving arms. May he/she rest in that place where there is no more pain. We thank you for all the moments of happiness and playfulness we shared with him/her, for the comfort and joy of his/her warm and furry body, and the way he/she enriched our lives with his/her beauty and his/her love over the years. And we pray too for ourselves. Our lives seem at this time full of sorrow and emptiness without him/her. Help us, O Lord, to trust in your promise that love will triumph over death. And we pray, in the name of Jesus, that Good Shepherd who cared for every one of his sheep, that at the last we may be reunited with him/her and all those we have loved.

A blessing

Almighty and protecting God, we ask you to bless us all, both men and beasts, for we are all your creatures. Watch over our friends the animals, those that live with men and those that live in the wild. Pour mercy and kindness into the hearts of all men that they may be gentle with those animals in their care. We pray especially for all creatures who are lost, sick, hungry, frightened or in pain. And we ask you to bring them at the last, with us, to your peace and rest.

Note

Non-Christians can leave out the reference to Jesus. For agnostics suitable readings might include a passage from *Memories* by John Galsworthy or one from the essays of Jerome K. Jerome. These and other poems about dogs can be found in *Faithful to the End* by Celia Haddon*. Other poems can be found in *The Neighbours* by Fougasse. Further prayers can be found in Bless *All Thy Creatures, Lord* by Richard Newman.

This service can, of course, be adapted for the death of any animal. For cats, the poem by Thomas Hardy (pages 152–153), or the one by the Reverend Potter (page 157) are probably the best.

* © Celia Haddon. Please feel free to use this compilation of prayers and readings. But if it is to be reproduced in print or any other media, other than National Canine Defence League Publications, permission to do so should be sought from Celia Haddon via www.celiahaddon.co.uk

Animal Souls

Do animals have souls you ask of me?
No, not as humans do in their degree,
But loved and loving beasts, the wise agree,
By body's death could never cease to be.

                                            Anon

Friend

Dear old dog — a little furry face
I hold you in a last embrace.
You, who never heard of sin —
Surely God will let you in?
And when I kneel outside the Gate
A penitent, awaiting fate,
God may shake His head and sigh,
Then, maybe, He'll catch your eye —
One melting glance, one plea from you
And God will laugh, and let me through.

                                    Yvonne Lynton

Message From a Little Ghost

I've explained to St Peter I'd rather stay here
Outside the Pearly Gate
I won't be a nuisance
I won't even bark
I'll be very patient and wait.

I'll lie here and chew a celestial bone,
No matter how long it may be.
I miss you so much,
If I went in alone,
It wouldn't be heaven to me.

Muriel Whitehead Jarvis

Courts of Heaven

High up in the courts of Heaven today
A little dog angel waits;
With other angels he will not play
But sits alone at the gate.
'For I know my master will come,' says he
'And when he comes he will call for me.'

And his master far on earth below,
As he sits in his easy chair,
Forgets sometimes — and he whistles low
For the dog that is not there.

And I know when at length his master waits
Outside in the dark and the cold,
For the hand of death to open the gate
And to lead to those courts of gold;
A little dog angel's eager bark,
Will comfort his soul in the shivering dark.

E.B.

A Question for St Peter

Will God let the creatures in,
Innocent and free from sin?

Heaven's gate is open wide
To those for whom our Saviour died,

And all repentant sinners claim
Free salvation in His name.

Brutal, callous, filled with greed,
Envious, selfish . . . own their need

And joyfully are welcomed in;
But what of beasts who do not sin?

Must their souls forever wait
Humbly outside Heaven's gate,

While their oppressors stream inside
Washed clean of blood, washed free of pride?

Words cannot tell the joy in Heaven
Over one ransomed soul forgiven,

But will God let His creatures in
Who suffer much but cannot sin?

Diana Salmond

A Small Black Ghost

How could I know a small black ghost
Would haunt each shadowed corner where,
In vibrant life he'd wait for me
To turn the key and enter there?

How could I ever dream that he
Would catch the corner of my eye,
Or brush against receding heel
As once he did; as I pass by?

How could I dream — or do I dream?
Is it my grief which conjures there,
Bright golden eyes alight with love
For just a second on the stair?

For when I turn, or fix my gaze,
There is no small bright ghost to see;
Only each ever-empty space,
As empty as the heart of me.

Nan Ford

For Lacey

She's gone. My faithful friend of many years,
My dog; she's dead; I've exhausted all my tears.
Now I walk alone. A wraith-like form I see,
A shadow? A trick of light? It must be
A conjured image of a heart that grieves.
But, the snap of twigs? The rustle of dead leaves
As she runs ahead, down the woodland track,
Then stops, tongue lolling, eyes bright, looking back.
The illusion fades, forlorn, I sit and rest.
A questing cold nose, on my hand is pressed.
I caress the silky head, the velvet ears;
A déjà vu? A memory of other years?
The warm weight of her head upon my knee
I feel; but she is dead. How can that be?

Daphne White

Chapter 9

Lost, Missing, Strayed – or Given Away

'People can suffer terribly when their pets go missing. I know of a Burmese cat which went missing from a boarding kennel and the owner was so upset she went temporarily blind. Then it was found happily living on a rubbish heap and her sight returned.'

Dr Mary Stewart

Some say that to worry over a missing pet is a worse experience than to mourn one that has died. It is impossible to grieve – because after all, Tibby, or whoever it is, might burst through your cat door any day of the week, the phone might ring and lo and behold, Spot has been collected by the police – or you might look up and see the budgie perching on the branch of a high sycamore.

What it *is* possible to do, unfortunately, is worry. Has the cat been taken by cunning vivisectionists? Has the dog been snatched by cruel tormentors who are at this very moment wreaking unspeakable tortures upon it? Is the budgie sitting on a windswept branch being sneered at by crows who *know* how to survive in the wild? Or is the pet just lost — bewildered, cold, starving, and longing, just longing, for home?

The imagination runs riot and frequently we impose our own personal fears on to the scenario — even though we have no idea, for instance, whether animals can 'long' for home in the way we do. Bewildered and cold they may be, but we don't even know if they experience being lost in the same way as us. And most of the time, anyway, our fantasies are just cockeyed. It is extremely unlikely that animals in this country are stolen by vivisectionists, and while there is a very, very remote chance a cat might be stolen for its fur, it would be swiftly and professionally dispatched, if it were, and its suffering probably less than if it were knocked down by a car and left to die in the gutter.

Pauline Martignetti, a driver with the Battersea Dogs & Dogs Home who spends her days picking up strays, says: 'If you lose your dog, nine times out of ten you will get it back. Most of the dogs do get to police stations eventually. Obviously in cases of very expensive dogs, some are picked up by unscrupulous characters who want to sell them, but to what extent it goes on I don't know. Those dogs who go to the police stations are kept there for twenty-four hours and then brought here where they're kept seven days before they go up for sale, unless they're claimed. And if they're not sold they're kept indefinitely.

'The vast majority of dogs are taken in by nice members of the public, a few are taken to the RSPCA and some are picked up by the increasing numbers of dog wardens. Only sometimes does a person just like the look of a lost dog, the dog gets attached to the person and gets taken home. You shouldn't really do that, of course, you should report the dog to the police so that they have a record of it, in case it does belong to someone else.'

How does she know whether a dog is a stray or whether it's just out for a walk on its own?

'If a dog looks pretty street-wise and is trotting along like a dog with a mission – if he looks as if he knows more about life than I do – then I'd leave him alone. But if they're in trouble with the traffic, about to get flattened, then we pick them up. Packs? They would form packs if they were allowed, but in London they're not given time. Usually if a dog is a stray it will be picked up within a couple of days.'

Even so, one man returned to the Battersea Dogs & Cats Home every week for a year to search for his missing pet.

Cats are much better survivors than dogs. Despite anxieties that Fluff is whimpering under a bush and dying of hunger, cats generally are much abler to return to the wild than dogs. If they're lost in the country they will survive on mice and small animals; in the town there is nearly always a feral community which they can join. Feral communities are reasonably welcoming about letting new strays in, so your cat, if it is missing, needn't be a paid-up member of the club with badge, tie and password to gain admittance. It is also said that an animal has an ability to 'decide to die' if life gets too much for it. It will not be hanging on for years, worn out with gloom, depression and starvation. If it just can't hack the life it's leading, it may well become more prone to disease or just curl up under a bush and not wake up.

When an animal goes missing, it's important to swing into action right away. Firstly, tell the police, the Blue Cross or RSPCA, the emergency vet hospitals, Cats Protection, local radio stations and so on.

Next call is to the local cleansing department to see if any bodies have been picked up by the roadsides – local councils keep records.

Then write out several large notices, with an enlarged photograph of the animal if possible, and pin these to nearby trees, railings and so on. Local shops can be helpful, too.

Lost cats will usually only roam around when there is no one about – so ask milkmen, postmen, newspaper deliverers and anyone else who's about at the crack of dawn, if they have spotted your pet. And ask around to see if there are any locked garages or sheds nearby. It could be that your animal might have wandered in there and got shut in. Many is the time that one of my animals has gone missing for a whole Bank Holiday or Easter and come back cross and blinking on Monday night – and since it's unlikely he has taken a weekend jaunt to Blackpool I can only assume he went somewhere and got locked in while a householder was away – and only got out when he returned.

If your animal is missing, he doesn't come back and you get stuck in a trough of anxiety that just won't go away, Dr Mary Stewart recommends holding a 'missing animal's funeral service' to help you put a full stop to your own unhappiness.

Had I known of the idea, I would have done this when my own cat, Gums, went missing. This is a letter I sent to a lovely lady who used to help bereaved pet owners by letter. I include it because it shows how worried one can get even about an animal one doesn't particularly like. I have not changed a word of it.

> I hope you don't mind my writing to you as a client as it were! But I am feeling very gloomy because I've lost one of our cats. Not the new one, Corky, who is fine, but the other one. He was/is a big tabby known as Gums, who we got far too young from his mother before we knew better. He'd never been handled by humans as his mother was wild, and it was dreadfully cruel of us to take him away from her at six weeks. He howled all the time he was here for about a week and never really recovered.
>
> The only person he would ever come near was me – whenever my partner or my son came into the room he

would usually shoot out. But if I was on the sofa he'd come up and sit near me, purring. Sometimes he'd come up to me and suckle my earlobe as if it was his mother's nipple. Rather disgusting but it obviously gave him comfort. He had bad breath and a horrible habit of chewing his food at the side of his mouth and he tended to wee in dribbles on cushions so you can imagine that only a mother (in this case me) could love him – and even I was hard-pressed. We did think once of giving him away because he was such a dud of a cat but when it came to it I felt so unhappy I couldn't bring myself to and we kept him. I felt that he was such a weird cat and it had been our fault really that he was like that and the least we could do would be look after him and love him as best we could. In a way he was like a disabled child.

Recently I took Corky to the vet to have him jabbed for cat flu and when the vet asked about the other cat I said honestly that the quicker he got cat flu the better as he was such an unhappy creature, really. We discussed him and the vet gave me some hormone pills which he said might calm him down a bit and I resolved to have a real go at Gums and feed him his pills and try to get him calmer and happier. I got one pill down him, sneaked into his food (he'd had them before so they didn't do him any harm) and we went away for the weekend, leaving him with my son, which has always been fine. We got back and he was here and then I sprayed the house for fleas, again on my vet's recommendation, and for some reason Gums took fright and shot out of the cat door. This was nothing new because, as you can imagine, he spent his entire time shooting out of the cat door in terror. But this time he didn't come back.

It's now been a week since he's gone. It's been a
particularly cold and freezing week and I can't help
thinking of him out there starving and cold. He's
completely unable to fend for himself and no one would
take him in, nor would he go in to anyone as he is such a
wretchedly frightened creature. I have been out night after
night in the streets all around us calling for him but he is so
peculiar I feel there is a chance he would be too frightened
to respond to my call. I've pinned notes to trees and some
people have called but no one has seen him. I have rung the
council but they rather annoyingly say that they have 'good
news – no cats have been swept up'. To me, of course this
is bad news. I would do anything to know that Gums was
dead. He would really be happier dead. I just hope against
hope that he was killed off in the cold weather. But then
'kind' friends tell me that cats are surprisingly resilient –
which is the last thing I want to hear.

It's the thought of him lost and hungry and longing for
home (I am sure I'm anthropomorphising here) that really
tears me up. If he were dead I would be quite happy. If he
came back I would be even happier. But I find it terribly
hard to bear the not knowing.

I don't really know what you can do except write me a
kind letter back. Or perhaps give me some advice on how
one might track him down. But just a reply would be very
nice because both my partner and my son, though very
sympathetic, don't really understand how I can feel about
such a non-cat. If you know anything of the chances of his
being dead of cold do please tell me. As I say I really don't
want to be told that cats are resilient and there's always
hope. I want to be reassured that it's extremely unlikely
he's alive and that no house-cat could survive in sub zero

temperatures without food for a week.

The lady wrote me back a lovely letter. She pointed out that Gums would probably have either died in the cold or have joined a feral community and, since he was basically a wild cat, he might be having more fun than he had at home. I felt much reassured.

There is a happy ending to this story. This is an entry from my diary:

> Guess who walked in today, his tail like a shoelace, his legs like pencils and his fur all sticking out? Gums! After being away two and a half months! Yesterday we'd just been ringing round rescue cat homes to get a new cat and now this. He is even madder than before and I can only say Denis [my partner] and Will [my son] were not wildly pleased to see him and even I had second thoughts. Where on earth has he been? His ribs are sticking out and his hips are practically showing and he ate four meals this morning and miaows for more whenever I see him. Am taking him to the vet tomorrow who I hope will be like Sherlock Holmes and be able to say: 'From the clay soil I find beneath his left claw, I would suggest he has been on a building site; from the feathers in his faeces, he has been living off birds, from his yellow tongue I deduce he has taken to smoking small cheroots, and from the stray red fibres attached to his tail I would hazard a guess that he has been sleeping on a sixteenth-century Turkish carpet. The small gun I find concealed about his undercarriage leads me to suspect he has been keeping bad company and the bald patches around his upper paws can only be the sign of shackles of a kind only to be found in a Moroccan prison.'

But knowing the vet, all he will say is 'That'll be fifty quid please.'

Poor, mad old Gums.

But maybe your pet's not missing. It's just that circumstances have meant that you have to part with it. Perhaps one of the family has an allergy, perhaps a new landlord won't countenance pets, it may be that the animal's behaviour has become erratic, it may not suit the presence of another, new pet, or perhaps you've had to move into a flat without a garden. Divorce is often a cause of having to part with much-loved pets – or perhaps the person who used to keep a dog company during the day when the owner worked, has moved or died and it would not be fair to leave the animal on its own. Perhaps you have got a job abroad, or you're ill, the pet doesn't get on with your new baby, you have to go into sheltered housing, you're broke – or perhaps you're just experiencing the loss of saying goodbye to a stray that you looked after on holiday.

All these 'goodbyes' can spark off tremendous anxieties and unhappiness. Will anyone else be able to understand the animal just like you did? Will it be taken for walks? Will it miss you as much as you miss it? Remember that if you have chosen your pet's new home carefully, and that it is well fed and loved, it will be happy. The new owner might miss a few tricks that you had spotted, but who knows, he or she might also spot aspects of your pet that you had missed. There will be disadvantages for your pet moving to a new home, but there may well be advantages for it as well.

This 'goodbye' loss is perhaps felt most deeply by those who use dogs as aids. Jill Nicholson is a psychologist who worked on research commissioned by Guide Dogs for the Blind Association, looking at how guide dog owners feel when they have to part with a dog that has been their eyes. Obviously if they can keep their dog, most guide dog owners will do their best to do so. But perhaps they can't afford it. Perhaps the new dog wouldn't get on with the old dog. Perhaps there's no one to be with the old dog when the owner's out with the new one and so on.

Taking on a new guide dog is difficult enough, without grieving for the old one as well. One guide dog owner described it as like 'getting a forced divorce from a beloved partner and re-marriage to someone unknown'.

'The thought of kicking him out after he had been such a good servant to me was hard to bear and I felt like a traitor,' said another.

Guide dogs are not just 'sight' for the blind person, they are more than a substitute pair of specs. They are seen as 'social facilitators' to use the jargon. In other words, when a blind or disabled person has a dog, the dog takes away from their disability in some way. A man in a wheelchair may be embarrassedly shunned in the street, but if that man has a dog many people will feel the dog gives them permission to come up and make contact, through the animal.

'The bond between guide dog owners and guide dogs is so intense,' says Jill Nicholson. 'We all love our pet dogs dearly and grieve when they go away or die, but my goodness it's nothing to what the guide dog owners feel when they've had this close companion for about seven years and then have to part from it. There is a different dimension when you're *working* with a dog, there is this two-way communication which is very different to the communication most people have with their animals. The dog becomes almost part of their identity. And with a dog they feel so much more confident in the ordinary world. Blind people will be shunned using a long cane, but with their guide dog it's a different matter.

'Some people are so upset when their guide dog gets too old to work that they can't retrain another dog. It is like a major bereavement. And losing the dog often reactivates the feelings they had when they went blind.'

Aine Wellard, a pet bereavement counsellor who is also blind, described how she felt when it was suggested her dog was 'past it' and would have to be returned to the Guide Dogs for the Blind Association or given away.

'My guide dog, Sherry, was a yellow Labrador and perhaps more importantly she was an inseparable part of my life,' she said. 'Sherry was two and a half years old when I got her and since then she had attended university with me, accompanied me to all my lectures and seminars; she was also present at my graduation ceremony. She had travelled on trains, boats, buses and planes with me. On one occasion she was even allowed into Buckingham Palace and was stroked by Prince Philip. For my veterinary surgeon, though, the past had no relevance to the present (or so it would have seemed) because when Sherry was in her tenth year my veterinary surgeon, offering no valid explanation, decided that it was time that she went to live with somebody else.

'I was confused because suddenly, without fully understanding why, I was being ordered to put the past behind me, sever the bond that existed between me and my dog and, like a sack of old rubbish, I was expected to give her away and immediately adjust to a life without her, as if she had never existed.'

Eventually she kept Sherry until she was put to sleep, was able to tackle her vet about his seemingly insensitive remarks and clear up what had apparently been a problem of communication.

Chapter 10

'You Can Always Get Another One ...'

'I couldn't be friends with any other . . . because he wouldn't
have known me before I was married, and wouldn't have
barked at Doady when he first came to the house . . . He
has known me in all that has happened to me . . .'
Dora refusing another dog to replace Jip in *David Copperfield*
by Charles Dickens.

The most hurtful thing a friend can say, when your pet has
died, is: 'You can always get another one.' Each word stabs
at the heart of the pet owner. 'Always' for instance.
Always? The bereaved pet owner's feelings are that she can *never*
replace her pet. And of course she's right. Her pet has died. It can
never return.

'Get' is another word that hurts the bereaved. It implies that you
can just go out and buy another dog in the same way as you might
'get' more sugar if you'd run out. You don't just 'get' a pet. 'Choose',
perhaps, or 'welcome into your family', but not 'get'. And finally, the

words 'another one' – as if all dogs, cats and birds were the same and one is no different to another.

The other word that's used, even by vets and bereavement counsellors, unfortunately, is 'replace'. 'Why not replace your dog?' they ask. And yet no one would suggest, if your partner died, that you could 'replace' him or her. It would be unthinkably insensitive.

Some pet owners feel they'd like a new animal as quickly as possible. Others feel that they just couldn't bear to love another one – partly because they'd feel disloyal to their old pet's memory and partly because they can't bear the prospect of going through the inevitable pain of parting with another pet when *it* dies, too.

However, there are lots of arguments *for* loving another animal – succinctly put by readers who got in touch with me after I had published a letter on the problem page from a woman who had written in saying that after her pet's death she could never give her heart to another animal again.

'The lady who wrote to you is obviously capable of a great deal of love for a pet so I would like to ask her to spread it around to some other poor creature,' she wrote. 'I know my old cat Samuel would be proud of me for the love I have given to my new Marmalade, although in my heart of hearts no one will ever take his place.'

> This is what a dead dog could say if it could: 'All dogs are different in that they each have their own little ways that endear them to those who love us. It may be some little games we play or tricks we learn or the way we look at you or some little thing about our appearance, like having one ear black and one white.
>
> 'While I was with you on earth, you grew to love me as I loved you. We both gave each other happiness and love. We do not stay on earth long and soon the time comes when we must pass on and make way for another of our kind who

also needs love and care, just as I did when you found me. I hope you loved me enough to make you love all dogs and to pass the love and care you gave me to another lonely dog. I know I will always have a special place in your heart and that special place will always be there. Another dog will never fill that place, but will find another place beside mine. If you loved me enough to make you want to give your love to another dog, I would be very proud as I would have fulfilled my mission on earth and saved another dog from loneliness. Thank you for your loving care and one day in another place in another world we will all be together again. And when you find another dog, give it all the love and care you gave me and then when its turn comes, too, to pass on, it will be as proud and happy for the life and love you gave it as I was and it will have loved you as I did.

'There are many of us in dogs' homes with no hope – looking for someone like you to love as I loved you. Please find one.'

Robin

After the death of my beloved Labrador I was devastated. I felt no human being could mean as much to me as she did. I was very out of patience with those who told me to 'get another dog'. Then I spoke to an elderly friend, a dog owner and dog lover. He told me a story about a stray dog who had eventually died 'without the touch of a gentle hand or loving word'. This really brought me to my senses, made me realise my dog had not been allowed to suffer and had always been loved and knew it. It also made me realise that all my tears were for myself because of my missing her. A dog may not have had any life at all but for its owner.

Selina

We never had children and when Bess died I felt as if I'd
lost a child. I thought I would burst with grief. When we
got another dog, Trixie, I could feel no love for it at all
and could only think of Bess. I cried each night thinking
the hurt would never go. Then one night as I sobbed into
my pillow I was aware I was being watched. I turned over
to see Trixie looking at me with big, sad eyes and she was
licking my hand. Her eyes seemed to say: 'Please don't cry,
if you give me a chance I'll help you to love me too.' For
the first time since I'd had her I cuddled her and realised
we needed each other and from that day on my love for
her grew and the pain of losing Bess eased.

Mirabel

No new pet can ever 'replace' the lost loved one, but they're loved
in different ways. In fact one survey showed that 75 per cent of pet
owners got a new pet within a year of the death of a pet.

My advice to anyone who has lost a pet is to replace them
and not to feel guilty. Even after all these years my family
still say: 'Do you remember when Cindy did this or Cindy
did that?' She might not be with us any more but we still
have lovely memories.

Fran

I did get another dog, Sam, a week after our Shep had died
– from a rescue kennels. I must admit getting Sam really
did help me, because you have to watch pups. And I had
problems with Sam because he had dysentery so it made it
harder to watch him. But we got him over that and now
he's part of the family. He's a year old now and still a bit
of a rogue, but it's the best thing I ever did. He is such a
loving dog, but nothing to compare with my Shep.

Sophie

One of my favourite letters came from a woman who was determined never to have another animal. She enclosed a poem she had written after her dogs died.

> *Two dogs I've had but no more now,*
> *I couldn't stand the ache*
> *Of saying: 'Yes it's time to go'*
> *My heart about to break.*
> *I feel the guilt so heavily*
> *And yet deep down I know,*
> *The only peace that they could get*
> *Was if I let them go.*
> *And so I'll go on trying*
> *To keep a smiling face,*
> *But never in my life will any*
> *Dog fill up their place.*

Oh, yeah? Two years later she was loving another dog – one she had rescued from a cruel family who were about to get it put down.

The same happened to Muffin's owner. When Muffin went missing, she couldn't bear the thought of loving another dog. A friend tried to persuade her, talking of a golden Labrador who was unwanted by its owners and in need of a good home.

> I said no straight away. People kept pushing dogs at me all
> the time. They couldn't seem to understand that Muffin
> could not be replaced like that. However, after a while I
> began to fuss other dogs. I mean I would stop, every time I
> saw a dog, to stroke it. It was just like a woman who's lost
> a child and every child is a reminder. I can remember one
> day as I stopped to stroke a dog and it happily wagged its
> tail. I knelt down and hugged it, oblivious to anyone

around, saying again and again: 'I love you, I love you.' As
I carried on stroking and hugging this dog, a lump came
into my throat and the tears began to well up inside me
like they never had before and they fell down my cheeks. It
was the first time I had been able to cry since Muffin
disappeared. Then a couple of months later, for some
strange reason, I started to think about this unknown dog
my friend had mentioned and I felt really protective and
sorry about her. She was on my mind the whole day. It felt
like a sign, a calling. It's hard to explain except it was like a
message from another world saying it was me who could
change her life. Then I felt it was time to accept the truth,
that I may never see Muffin again, not in this life anyway.
My friend brought the dog round to see me and when I
spoke to her she jumped at me giving me a wash. We've
been together ever since.

Katie Boyle is adamant that a bereaved pet owner should take on
a new pet. 'It's so desperately selfish not to, because there are so
many dogs in need of a home. If you have a good home and are
capable of bonding with a dog – have another! Otherwise you are
being just so selfish. The penalty for loving is always high. Nothing
is going to last for ever. There are so many animals suffering – and
by not taking in a dog, you are letting another dog who needs a
home go to a bad home, be unhappy, become another stray and be
another casualty. I think that is wrong.'

Some owners are elderly and naturally they are anxious about
taking on a new pet. They couldn't bear to face another
bereavement – but, worse, what if they, the owner, died first? It
wouldn't be fair . . . the pet couldn't cope.

But Averil Jarvis, of the Cinnamon Trust, says: 'When an elderly
person loses an animal the pain can be incredibly acute. Particularly

as they often feel they can't replace it. But this is where we step in. We say – go on, have a dare, have a smaller one, have an elderly one. And we ask them to look at it in a different way. Not at the heartache they're going to have if it dies, but we ask them to look at the animal and the love it needs now. Okay, it might die, but if it dies, do it again. You will have shared love for a few years and that makes such a difference. Look how much *they* need *you* rather than the other way around. Love doesn't die, love goes on.'

Elderly people would be unwise to take on a puppy, and families should always be careful about taking a new dog into their families when there's an old, dying dog around. It might be nice for the family, but the old dog might well feel depressed and threatened and realise intuitively that this new puppy is indeed a replacement – being brought in before the old pet's time is up. If you want to make a smooth transition, get a new puppy *before* your original dog or cat gets old and ill.

Bereaved owners often go to Battersea Dogs & Cats Home to search for a new pet. 'But if someone's too upset I might tell them to wait before getting a dog,' says one of the volunteers. 'We vet everyone before we let them buy a new dog. We ask them what happened to their last dog and sometimes they break down, burst into tears and can't say why their dog died. If they're too upset we might say: "Do you really think you're ready for another dog?"

'But sometimes they miss their dog and they want to replace what they've lost exactly – they want a dog of the same size, colour and breed. This doesn't usually work and they often bring it back saying: "It's not the same", or "It's too early", or "It doesn't chew slippers in the same way the old one did".

'The people I don't like dealing with are the ones who say: "I had my dog put down this morning and I want a new one right away." It shows they haven't got a shred of emotion, and they're treating the dog as if it were a new pair of shoes. You generally find these people aren't really suitable dog owners anyway and their last dog wasn't treated that well.

'But some people who come here have waited years before they get a new dog. I do sometimes advise them to go for something completely different – different breed, different colour and so on.'

But some people are adamant that they will never get another one:

> Our dog now lies in a corner of our garden. I always fed
> him, exercised him and loved him, he gave me back that
> love so many times over. Many people would not
> understand how a grown man of sixty-two could be so soft
> about a dog but they have never given love to a dog or
> received it. I cry as I write nine months later. I cannot go
> out and get another. He was my true friend.
>
> Johnny

If you're someone who feels they could never get another animal, here are some compromise suggestions – which means you could give animals love without taking on the major responsibility of pet ownership.

> I could never have another dog. I now only keep fish – but
> even so I mourn their loss as little individual characters'
> lives because I love all animals, however insignificant.
>
> Trevor

> I still miss my little cats, especially the old one, but am
> kept well occupied by my family of waifs and strays which
> has now risen to five cats, two dogs, several hedgehogs and
> a collection of wild birds. One of the dogs travels about
> one and a half miles from a farm to get here. Heaven

knows how he found me – there must be a sign on the gate
saying Free Grub!

Valerie

I am a widow and when I lost my dog I thought I was too
old to have another. So now I look after the dogs of
relatives and friends when they are away or, if they're not
well, I walk them. It suits us all well – and they often look
in when they're passing. I don't ask for money but it is a
bonus to have them on loan for love and fuss.

Stella

Dr Mary Stewart says: 'What I feel is that there are two things
people lose when an animal dies. They lose their loving friend, but
they also lose something else which is what I call their "dogness" or
"catness". This is simply the presence of an animal around the
house. This *is* replaceable – the need to get up in the morning to
feed it, the walks, the patter of paws, the routine of having an
animal. And therefore if you can see getting a new animal as this to
start with, then you can worry about its personality later, which will
grow on you.'

Taking on a new pet, if you are elderly, may bring up a lot of
anxieties. If you die first, how do you ensure that it will be looked
after? It's essential you make very clear plans about what you want
to happen to your pet, and make them clear long before you die, not
just in your will – it may be too late for your wishes to be considered
by the time it's read. Tell your best friends, home helps, relations or
anyone near to you exactly what your wishes are. Because remember,
although a pet is a possession, a part of your estate, someone has to
feed it and care for it only hours after your death.

'The saddest thing is when the owner dies and the dog is whisked
into the police station and brought down here and it's done nothing

wrong, it doesn't know what's happening,' says Pauline Martignietti of Battersea Dogs & Cats Home. 'Often they're older dogs, they don't have a great chance of being sold since they're frequently fat and old and spoiled, doddery old mongrels. You can just see them thinking, as they sit here in one of our compounds: "What the hell have I done?" People should always make provision for their dogs in their will.'

Your pet is your possession so you can't leave any money to it, any more than you could leave money to your car. But you can leave your pet to someone and put them under an obligation to look after it, as long as they are agreeable. They may be more amenable if you provide the funds for them to do so. It may sound simple but the law is such that you'd really have to talk to a solicitor about all the ins and outs of doing this. You could make a legally binding contract with an organisation like the Cinnamon Trust or Cats Protection or Pro Dogs which means the organisation will look after your pet. Obviously a legacy of some kind in your will is always appreciated. Another method is to leave a 'carrot' for someone to look after your animal. In other words, to leave so much per year to someone on condition that your pet is looked after. You can keep this going per year.

Cats Protection will take in cats, but their policy is, rightly, to re-home as many as possible – otherwise their cat sanctuaries would be full, and anyway, as they point out, a cat's place is in the home, loved and cherished by a caring owner.

'We have had some dreadful examples of relatives behaving very badly to pets after their owners have died. The thing to remember is that relatives have no right to do anything with the animal because in law an animal is property. So you can't legally take a pet and have it put down while the owner is in hospital any more than you could go round to a person's house, ransack it and dispose of everything. But people are very funny about pets.

'One thing I don't like is owners saying they want their pets put to sleep on their death. If you provide an acceptable alternative, and they still have life more or less as they used to know it, they come to terms with their owners' death. We often have very old animals coming here, sixteen and seventeen year olds. Of course it's probably different to the life they used to lead at home, but they have the company of other animals, they may have better walks and treats, so life isn't too bad at all.

'I always say, give them a chance. If they could go on to live their natural span happily, why not let them?'

So – the word for the future is simply: make adequate provision for any pet you have in your will, telling as many people about your plans as possible.

And secondly, if you have lost a pet, don't close the door to having another one, even if you have to wait. There are so many unwanted animals out there who need our love. Desperately.

Last Words To a Dumb Friend

Pet was never mourned as you,
Purrer of the spotless hue,
Plumy tail, and wistful gaze,
While you humoured our queer ways,
Or outshrilled your morning call
Up the stairs and through the hall -
Foot suspended in its fall —
While, expectant, you would stand
Arched, to meet the stroking hand,
Till your way you chose to wend
Yonder, to your tragic end.

Never another pet for me!
Let your place all vacant be;
Better blankness day by day
Than companion torn away.
Better bid his memory fade
Better blot each mark he made
Selfishly escape distress
By contrived forgetfulness,
Than preserve his prints to make
Every morn and eve an ache.

From the chair whereon he sat
Sweep his fur, nor wince thereat;
Rake his little pathways out
Mid the bushes roundabout;
Smooth away his talons' mark
From the claw-worn pine-tree bark,
Where he climbed as dusk enbrowned

Waiting us who loitered round.

Strange it is this speechless thing,
Subject to our mastering,
Subject for his life and food
To our gift, and time, and mood;
Timid pensioner of us Powers
His existence ruled by ours
Should by crossing at a breath
Into safe and shielded death,
By the merely taking hence
Of his insignificance —
Loom as largened to the sense,
Shape as part, above man's will
Of the Imperturbable.

As a prisoner, flight debarred,
Exercising in a yard,
Still retain I, troubled, shaken,
Mean estate, by him forsaken;
And this home which scarcely took
Impress from his little look,
By his faring to the Diam,
Grows all eloquent of him.

Housemate I can think you still
Bounding to the window-sill,
Over which I vaguely see
Your small mound beneath the tree,
Showing in the autumn shade
That you moulder where you played.

Thomas Hardy

My Will

When humans die, they make a will
To leave their homes and all they have
to those they love.
I, too, would make a will if I could write.
To some poor wistful, lonely stray
I leave my happy home,
My dish, my cosy bed, my cushioned chair, my toy.
The well loved lap, the gentle stroking hand,
the loving voice,
The place I made in someone's heart,
The love that at the last could help me to
a peaceful painless end
Held in loving arms.

If I should die, Oh do not say,
'No more a pet I'll have,
to grieve me by its loss'
Seek out some lonely, unloved dog
And give my place to him.
This is the legacy I leave behind —
'tis all I have to give.

Anon

Chapter 11

―⦂⦂⦂―

In Memoriam

Although I've changed the names of their owners, these are the names of the dogs, cats, rats, sparrows, budgies, hamsters and guinea pigs whose stories have appeared in the book. I'd like to say a big thank you to all the owners who wrote in to tell me about their feelings — and their pets.

Mini	Minky	Tich	Sparrow Charlie
Tibby	Woodbine	Shep	Pavsta
Goldy	Rebel	Louie	Sam
Boney	Shaney	Rusty	Skipper
Suki	Meg	Bob	Lassie
Holly	Fred	Snowy	Smokey
Korky	Arco	Dandy	Candy
Blueboy	Mitzi	Dougal	Gus
Tinker	Mandy	Gin	Toby
Susie	Lady	Sammy	Pixie
Muffin	Harvey	Keaton	Patsy
Barney	Felix	Becky	Bramble

Dusty	Leo	Cally	Sherry
Emma	Lucy	Rex	Sindy
Susan	Gizmo	Kitty	Havoc
Sparky	Tiddles	Wellington	Bimbo
Sadie	Katy	Trix	Fudge
Chum	Feather	Bodie	Sabbie
Snoopy	Whisky	Trixie	Sally
Patch	Goldie	Bonnie	Penny
Ben	Buffy	Judy	Tansy
Stacy	Chester	Barney	Bobby
Lucky	Tigger	Honey	Brandy
Bess	Gypsy	Sheba	Jimmy
Cindy	Princess	Teddy	Samuel
Mikky	Peter	Boomer	Kabre
Brownie	Prince	Lacey	Perry
Jess	Candy	Nick	Fat Ada
Sooty	Bosscat	Toodie	Oscar
Emily	Galaxy	Mitzie	Boysie
Beefy	Chester	Mattie	Corky
Gums	Oscar		

To My Cat

You have a life of your own
I know:
And I can only guess
In what pathless wilderness
Your catly imagination heads
Beyond those humanised flowerbeds:
But sooner or later
I know
You'll find your way home.

I have a life of my own
You know:
And only a strange surmise
In those curious boot-button eyes
Can follow me through the closing door
Into the world's unresting road:
And sooner or later
You know
I'll find my way home.

For there is a life that we share
We two:
When we sit beside the fire
And our random thoughts conspire
To carry us back, both cat and Man
To that far-off garden where life began
And sooner or later
We know
We shall find our way home.

Reverend Charles Potter

Useful Addresses

The Pet Bereavement Support Service is run by the Society for Companion Animal Studies in conjunction with Blue Cross animal welfare charity.
Telephone helpline (8.30am – 8.30pm): 0800 096 6606
Website:
www.bluecross.org.uk/web/site/AboutUs/PetBereavement/PBSS Intro.asp
Email support: pbssmail@bluecross.org.uk

Children and pet loss
The Blue Cross and the Society for Companion Animal Studies produce an excellent booklet for children when a pet dies. You can download it online by going to: http://www.bluecross.org.uk/web/FILES/PBSS_and_memorials/Children_and_Pet_Bereavem ent_Leaflet_2008.pdf

There are any number of pet bereavement books for children on Amazon.com – put in the words 'pet bereavement children' – but the two delightful ones recommended by Blue Cross are *Goodbye Mog* by Judith Kerr (Picture Lions) and *Fred* by Posy Simmons (Young Puffin)

Ease Pet Bereavement Service

The EASE Preparing for Pet Loss programme is an email service for people who anticipate the loss of a beloved pet. They offer free support prior to, during and after expected loss. Website: www.ease-animals.org.uk

Animal Samaritans Pet Bereavement Service

Telephone helpline: 020 8303 1859
Website: www.animalsamaritans.org.uk/bereave.htm

Missing Pets Bureau

Website: http://www.missingpetsbureau.com

Newsletter

Departed Friend
5 Muirfield, Luton, Beds LU2 7SB
Tel: 01582 512184
Email: departedfriend@btinternet.com

Debby, the editor, will counsel bereaved pet owners by letter or email.

PRO Dogs

PRO Dogs Direct, 126 Davenport Road, Catford,
London SE6 2AS
Website: www.prodogsdirect.org.uk

They have a register of dogs looking for new homes.

Cats Protection

They have a register of cats needing a home.
Website: www.cats.org.uk

Battersea Dogs & Cats Home
There are three homes, in Battersea, Old Windsor and Brands
Hatch. For more information about rescue animals, go to:
www.dogshome.org

Cinnamon Trust
10 Market Square, Hayle, Cornwall TR27 4HE
Tel: 01736 757900

A charity devoted to caring for animals after their owners have
died.

The Association of Private Pet Cemeteries and Crematoria
Nunclose, Armathwaite, Carlisle CA4 9TJ
Tel: 01252 844478
Website: www.appcc.org.uk
Email: contact@appcc.org.uk

Cambridge Pet Crematorium
A505 Main Road, Thriplow Heath, Nr Royston, Herts SG8 7RR
Tel: 01763 207700
Website: www.cpccares.com

Animal artists and pet memorials
Animal artists and pet memorials are advertised in *Dogs Today*.
Tel: 01276 858880
Website: www.dogstodaymagazine.co.uk

Freezing
Website: www.cryonics.org/pets.html

Taxidermists
Get Stuffed, 105 Essex Road, London N1 2SL
Tel: 020 7226 1364
Website: www.thegetstuffed.co.uk
Animal Instincts
Website: www.animalinstinctsart.co.uk